GOLD UNDER
FIRE

GOLD UNDER
FIRE

The Christian & Adversity

GARY CRANDALL

Foreword by John C. Whitcomb

Pleasant Word

A Division of WINEPRESS PUBLISHING

Printed in the United States of America

Packaged by Pleasant Word, a division of WinePress Publishing, PO Box 428, Enumclaw, WA 98022. The views expressed or implied in this work do not necessarily reflect those of Pleasant Word, a division of WinePress Publishing. Ultimate design, content, and editorial accuracy of this work are the responsibilities of the author.

Unless otherwise noted, all Scriptures are taken from the New King James Version, © 1979, 1980, 1982 by Thomas Nelson, Inc., Publishers. Used by permission.

Scripture references marked KJV are taken from the King James Version of the Bible.

Scripture references marked NASB are taken from the New American Standard Bible, © 1960, 1963, 1968, 1971, 1972, 1973, 1975, 1977 by The Lockman Foundation. Used by permission.

ISBN 1-4141-0331-X
Library of Congress Catalog Card Number: 2004098524

This book is dedicated
To my Lord, who suffered for me
and
To my wife, Sherrie, who suffered with me

TABLE OF CONTENTS

FOREWORD
BY JOHN C. WHITCOMB, TH.D.

Sooner or later, to some extent or other, affliction (the sufferings which God plans for His people by which He accomplishes goals and purposes that otherwise could not be accomplished) will come into the life of every true believer. God's infallible Word is very clear on this (e.g., John 16:33; Acts 14:22; Rom. 8:36; Phil. 1:28–29, and 2 Tim. 2:8–13).

The question, then, is not whether, but when, where, and how affliction may come to us in the wisdom and mercy of our God. And an even bigger question is: how will I respond?

Our gracious God makes no mistakes with His children. He plans for each one of us exactly what we need and can bear in order that we may learn obedience. If our divine and sinless Lord had to learn obedience by the things which He suffered (Heb. 5:8), how can we claim exemption?
In recent months God has chosen to bring into the life of my wife and me physical and emotional affliction we have never known before. We take this to be a token of His special attention and love. One of the ways He has brought encouragement to us during these days is through reading this outstanding book by my former student and dear friend, Gary Crandall, pastor of the Berean Bible Church, Olathe, KS.

Gary and his wife Sherrie have also experienced deep affliction. Though he was an excellent student in theological seminary, he has not written this book from an "ivory tower" of academic theory alone. He has searched the Holy Scripture on a daily basis for many years and has applied its eternal truths to his own life first of all.

PREFACE
TO 2ND EDITION

Since the first publication of *Gold Under Fire* in 1993, the Lord has allowed me, in His infinite grace and wisdom, to have cause to personally apply all that I had previously written. Like Paul, albeit not to the same degree, I have been ". . . in afflictions, in hardships, in distresses . . ." (2 Cor. 6:4). These came upon me concurrent with the publication of this work and have shadowed me since. Not missing this connection, I have more than once thought that my next book shall be *How to be Healthy, Wealthy, and Wise (and may the Lord smite me with it!)*. But the Lord has not allowed me to write such a book, nor has He laid those desires (excepting in the spiritual realm) upon my heart.

My purpose in communicating this is not to complain. Far from it. For I have seen the Lord respond to my plight with hitherto unknown grace and divine enablement and peace beyond comprehending – all of which I may well have missed had my life not gone the path He had ordained for me. God's faithful hand has placed me in the furnace of affliction, and there He has guarded and guided me to the place of seeing only Him. I would not trade that for any amount of lessening of the affliction. My only prayer is that the gold He is refining in me will, indeed, by and by come to reflect the image of the Refiner.

I am also very grateful for the way God has used this book to minister

11

to the lives of so many. It is both amazing and humbling to hear from distant lands or prison confines or hospital beds or lonely homes how God has both glorified Himself and brought hope and direction to His people. It is my earnest prayer that as this second edition goes forth it will bear such fruit again and bring great honor to Whom all honor is due—our Lord and Savior, Jesus Christ.

In this you greatly rejoice, though now for a little while, if need be, you have been grieved by various trials, that the genuineness of your faith, being much more precious than gold that perishes, though it is tested by fire, may be found to praise, honor, and glory at the revelation of Jesus Christ.

(1 Peter 1:6–7)

PART ONE

Why Christians Suffer

It was barely dawn as the women set about their grim task. The burial spices they had prepared the day and evening before constituted their precious cargo. Perhaps they tried to brace themselves for the awful sight which most assuredly awaited them: the scarred body of their dead Lord. What they found instead seemed for the moment even more disastrous. The stone was rolled away and the body of Jesus was gone. "Why?!" resounded in their already broken hearts.

Looking back on this resurrection event through enlightened eyes, we see a glorious moment. We realize the victory that was won there. We celebrate this event dramatically every spring. We may have a hard time identifying with the feeling of perplexity these women experienced.

A careful look at Luke 24:4 may help us understand these women and ourselves better. The verse explains what was happening inside their hearts and minds. We are told: "And it happened, as they were greatly perplexed about this, that behold, two men stood beside them in shining garments." We are chiefly concerned with the word "perplexed." It is the English translation of a Greek word that means literally "to be without a way." It was used in a variety of fashions to indicate being at a loss, in doubt, or uncertain.[1] If we plug this idea back into the verse, we begin to see the frustration these women experienced. Something terrible had happened and they were at a loss. They were completely "without a way" to explain the empty tomb. The overbearing question which loomed before them was why? Why? Why?!

In my years as a pastor I have been asked that question more than any other. I have asked it myself more than once. It is a frank and often frustrating admission on our part that we are "without a way" to explain what has transpired in our lives.

In my first year as a pastor, the husband and father of a family in the church died. They knew he was in heaven. They knew his suffering was over. They knew God was with them. But all that knowledge did not answer their "whys." Why did he have to die *now*? Why did he have to die in that manner? Why did he have to leave them? Why did God allow it to happen? Why did they have to go through this? As I was bombarded with these questions, I could only offer a lamentable "I don't know" and wonder myself why such things happen. I felt like a man in a cave looking for a star. In knew that the answers, if they existed at all, did not lie within me. Although I had wondered "why" before, now my search began in earnest to discover both the answer to "why" and the way to respond.

Is it okay to ask "why"? Before we answer that question, we need to understand that it is *not* okay to question God's goodness or knowledge or judgment or power. We must agree with the Psalmist that "As for God, His way is perfect" (Psalm 18:30). It is *not* okay to substitute knowledge for faith. Ultimately, what is most important is not that *we* know but that *God* knows. It is *not* okay if our attitude is one of demanding instead of humble request. Our goal must be to bring into focus God's purpose, not to call into question God's authority. Beyond such limits, however, the question "why" is not only appropriate, it is often necessary. Was it important for the women to know why the tomb was empty? Yes! It was part of God's plan for them. Notice that they had the privilege of being the first ones to proclaim the risen Lord!

We may not always be able to understand "why." That, however, is based upon our own limitations and does not invalidate the question. In fact, since God often uses adversity as a teaching tool, it is helpful to ask, "why am I experiencing this difficulty?"

The quest before us is not for more information. The quest is to know God better, to seek to discern His purpose, and to "grow in the grace and knowledge of our Lord and Savior Jesus Christ" (2 Peter 3:18).

In this section, we offer some possible solutions to why Christians suffer. We do not suggest that there are no other possibilities, but this list will cover most situations. These suggested reasons are not mutually exclusive. That is, it is not a matter of narrowing it down to one or the other. In fact, it would be normal to find two and perhaps more of these possibilities in operation at the same time. The possible reasons for adversity, which we shall examine one at a time, include:

1. Sin in general
2. Individual sin
3. The prevention of pride
4. To learn God's ways
5. To learn patience
6. To learn to comfort others
7. That God might be glorified
8. Demonic activity
9. Unexplained and unknown reasons

To each believer who travels through the darkness of adversity, Christ has proclaimed Himself to be the One who came "to give them beauty for ashes, the oil of joy for mourning, the garment of praise for the spirit of heaviness; that they may be called trees of righteousness, the planting of the Lord, that He may be glorified" (Isaiah 61:3).

Although there is comfort in knowing that others share in the same kinds of sufferings we do, only the Word brings hope and only Christ brings victory. Therefore, this book is not a compilation of stories connected together with some verses but rather a presentation of biblical truth illustrated with some stories. Our ultimate goal in this study is to experience "the oil of joy for mourning . . . that He might be glorified."

BECAUSE OF SIN IN GENERAL

As a new believer, I tried to witness to a co-worker. As I sought to explain that God loved this man, he shot back angrily, "if God is a God of love, then why was my baby born with a cleft palate?" I was taken back. Being so inexperienced, I fell into the trap of trying to justify God and get Him out of a jam. Quite honestly, I did not know how to answer. I was frustrated by the dilemma. I could not deny the pain this man felt; I could not deny the love and grace of God. "What *was* the answer?" haunted me. "If God is sovereign, then why was my grand-daughter born with a cleft palate?" This question, coming years after the first one, threw me in a different way. For one thing, I was struck by the similarity of both the ailment involved and the anger of the speaker. More upsetting, however, was that this question was being asked by an acquaintance of mine who was the pastor of a large church!

Both of these men had experienced similar problems. Both were angry and hurt by what had happened to a precious baby girl in their lives. But there was one main difference which became important in solving this problem: the first man was a nonbeliever; the second man was a believer. The nonbeliever did not experience this tragedy just because of his nonbelief. The believer was not immune to this tragedy just because of his belief. What had befallen one had befallen the other.

Why? Because we live in a sin-sick world with a cursed environment. This planet is cursed because of original sin and because we are all "by nature children of wrath, just as the others" (Ephesians 2:3).

This is a large part of the answer to the question "why." It is not, however, the answer to the *problem* (i.e., "what can be done about it?"). That important topic will be addressed later. For now, let's examine what God has to say about why sin has such an effect on our lives and our world.

"The Lord God commanded the man, saying, 'Of every tree of the garden you may freely eat; but of the tree of the knowledge of good and evil you shall not eat, for in the day that you eat of it you shall surely die'" (Genesis 2:16–17). This death was brought about, not because the tree of knowledge bore poisonous fruit, but because of the disobedience associated with eating the fruit.[2] Sin leads to death. As James wrote: "Then, when desire has conceived, it gives birth to sin; and sin, when it is full-grown, brings forth death" (James 1:15). This death is first of all, in its most drastic and horrible form, separation from God. This spiritual death has as its only cure and hope the blood of Christ. The reader is referred to the entire second chapter of Ephesians and especially verses 1, 5, and 12–13. Although the spiritual death is much more critical, it is the physical death which is more the focus of this present study.

That physical death, as well as spiritual death, was intended in Genesis 2:17 becomes readily apparent from Genesis 3:17–19. Of particular interest, we note the last part of verse 19, which reads: ". . . till you return to the ground, for out of it you were taken; for dust you are, and to dust you shall return." Part of the curse upon Adam is that he would one day die. At least part of the reason God drove Adam out of the garden of Eden was to prohibit him from partaking of the tree of life "lest he put out his hand and take also of the tree of life, and eat, and live forever" (Genesis 3:22). In fact, no one was allowed access to this tree (Genesis 3:24). That Adam and his near descendants lived for long periods of time (Adam lived 930 years, Seth 912 years, Enoch 905 years, etc.) was a testimony to the state of perfection in which Adam was created. Also, whereas we have a history of disease in our ancestry (consider for instance all of the heredity illnesses), Adam had none. Ultimately, however, the concern is not how long we shall live, but the fact that we shall die. The curse upon Adam has fallen upon us. "Therefore, just as through one man sin entered the world, and death through sin, and thus death spread to all men, because all sinned." (Romans 5:12). The curse has fallen on us all. None of us have the right to point an angry finger at Adam "because all sinned." We have less right to blame God for our troubles than an arsonist has to blame the fire chief for the smoldering rubble of the building he torched.

Why do Christians suffer? One reason is that we live in a sin-filled world. Our bodies bear the curse of Adam and we are in the process of dying. Dying in most cases will involve some sort of suffering. In addition, because we have imperfect bodies, the genes we have received and those we transmit are corrupted. This results in defects, some of which are obvious at birth (eleven toes, cleft palate, etc.) and others which take longer to discern (lower IQ, poor vision, etc.). We all have numerous defects. The wonder is not that such defects exist, but that they are not more severe, obvious, and prevalent. Also, we live in relatively close proximity to many other sinners. Because of our sinful self-centered nature, we rob, murder, terrorize, cheat, and, in general, bring destruction and pain upon one another. Much of the suffering in this world, both by Christians and non-Christians, comes from the hands of our fellow sinful men and women.

An elderly widow who has her life's savings consumed by a con artist knows this truth. A mother who loses a son in battle knows this truth. A husband who loses his wife in an accident caused by a drunk driver knows this truth. A child who is born with a serious defect because the mother was an addict knows this truth. Through the pervasiveness of sin, we are destroying one another.

It was not mankind alone that was cursed in the garden. This planet also felt the sting of sin. In Genesis 3:17, God told Adam "cursed is the ground for your sake." This was not a temporary curse which the earth would outgrow. Indeed, all of creation still groans and will continue to suffer until the end when God will restore all things. The reader is referred to Romans 8:18–23 and Acts 3:21. Among other things, we find the statement that "the whole creation groans and labors with birth pangs together until now" (Romans 8:21). The earth, in a sense, suffers. We can see in such events as earthquakes, floods, volcanoes, and hurricanes the self-destructive suffering of the earth. Part of man's curse is that he is self-destructive; the same is true for the earth. We know, of course, that these kinds of disasters affect much more than the earth itself. Man not only causes the earth to suffer (through pollution, for example), but the earth, being cursed, inflicts suffering upon man. Since this planet is cursed itself, and since it is occupied by sin-filled and cursed people, the natural consequence is adversity and suffering.

That natural disasters fall upon Christians and non-Christians alike is evident both by experience and by the explanation of our Lord that "He makes His sun rise on the evil and on the good, and sends rain on the just and on the unjust" (Matthew 5:45). In this verse the emphasis is on good things (sun and rain), but the principle still holds. We cannot expect a hurricane to hit only pagans. We cannot expect a cold, or virus, or cancer to attack only the unsaved. We cannot expect an earthquake to divide the sheep from the goats or the wheat from the tares. We can expect trouble. Jesus said, "In the world you will have tribulation" (John 16:33). Consider this personal account by M. R. DeHaan II:

> Following the terrible Mexico City earthquake of 1985, live satellite coverage carried the news of Mexico's anguish to a watching world. I remember sitting in front of our television set stunned by the extent of the damage. Mountains of broken concrete filled the screen. Rescue workers dug frantically. Fires raged. Smoke and dust filled the air. Then suddenly in the lower left-hand corner of the screen appeared the words "Courtesy: SIN." The letters S-I-N actually stood for Spanish International Network, but for a moment it meant something different to me. It reminded me that in some way all trouble, pain, and suffering can be traced back to the problem of sin.

Christians suffered in that earthquake as well as non-Christians. Sin exacts a high price and it is no respecter of persons.

The scenario is not a pleasant one. God does not take sin lightly. It was necessary for God, as the Holy Judge, to condemn sin and to pass the judgment. But the story does not end on a bitter note. God not only judges perfectly, He loves perfectly. Even in the verse quoted above (John 16:33), the emphasis is really on hope. In its entirety it says:

"These things I have spoken to you, that in Me you may have peace. In the world you will have tribulation; but be of good cheer, for I have overcome the world." Wherever you find the note of curse you find the song of hope and love. Going back to Romans 8, we find much to celebrate about. Yes, it says that the total creation is cursed and we suffer along with it. But verse 18 says that "the sufferings of this present time are not worthy to be compared with the glory which shall be revealed in us." As verse 21 says, "the creation itself also will be delivered from the bondage of corruption into the glorious liberty of the children of God." The theme of Romans 8:23–25 is that there is hope!

My sister, Kathy, was born with a congenital disorder (Downs' Syndrome) which resulted in mental retardation. I used to feel sorry for her, but not anymore. She has family and friends who love her. Her own love and loyalty toward others could teach us much. She doesn't worry about the national budget deficit, taxes, or the threat of nuclear war. She does cry, however, when someone else gets hurt. She will one day depart from this life and the imperfect frame in which she was procreated. She will, by God's grace and mercy, put on a new, eternal and incorruptible body. All wounds will be healed on that glorious day.

We live in a sin-sick world. It hurts, and so do we. But if an earthquake should destroy our home, we know that we have a better home awaiting us (John 14:2–3). If a flood should wash away our business, we know that our treasure is in heaven (Matthew 6:25–34). If our friends should turn their backs on us and perhaps even mistreat us, we know that our closest friend, our precious Lord, will never leave us or forsake us (Hebrews 13:5). Even if a spouse has broken a promise of love and commitment, we know that God loves us with an everlasting love (Jeremiah 31:3), and He is always faithful (2 Timothy 2:13). If our bodies should give way to disease and death, we know that God has an immortal and incorruptible body awaiting us (1 Corinthians 15:53–54 and 2 Corinthians 5:1), and that "We are confident, yes, well pleased rather to be absent from the body and to be present with the Lord" (2 Corinthians 5:8).

The effects of both original sin and the pervasiveness of sin in general are so widespread as to account for, at least in part, every instance of adversity and suffering in this world. If you are suffering, it is because of sin. That is not to say that you are suffering as a direct result or consequence of your own personal sin (a possibility which will be addressed in the next chapter), but you are suffering because sin entered the world and brought with it adversity, sickness, and death. Sin is the mother of all suffering. There may be (and often are) other reasons for the difficulties we experience, but sin is always a factor.

Let us not dwell with remorse on the failure in the Garden of Eden by the first Adam. Let us instead rejoice in the victory won in the garden of Gethsemane by the second Adam. Let us not gaze at the tree with the forbidden fruit, but let us fix our eyes upon the tree of Calvary. Let us not look back to the closed door of Eden, but let us look forward to the torn veil and the open door to heaven. "In the world you shall have tribulation; but be of good cheer, I have overcome the world."

BECAUSE OF INDIVIDUAL SIN

In the late 1700s a minister was riding through a section of the state of South Carolina where custom forbade innkeepers to take payment from the clergy who stayed with them. The minister in question took supper without prayer and ate breakfast without prayer or grace and was about to take his departure when his host presented him the bill. "Ah, sir, I am a clergyman," said the minister. The landlord responded, "But you came here, smoked like a sinner, ate and drank like a sinner, and slept like a sinner; and now, sir, you shall pay like a sinner." Some Christians have the mistaken idea that since we belong to God, and since Jesus already paid the penalty for all of our sins, then individual sins are not and cannot be held against us. In other words, God would not in any way hold us accountable for sins that Christ has already paid for. In this chapter we will examine two reasons why adversity and suffering may be directly related to individual sin. They are (1) the practical results of sin, and (2) the chastisement of the Father.

What, however, shall we say to the charge that since "Jesus paid it all" we have nothing to pay? The answer is this: Jesus paid for all of our sins in a judicial sense. That is, we will not come under judgment for our sins since we have (present tense) everlasting life, and will not come into judgment (a promise for the future), but rather have passed (accomplishment in the past) from death into life (John 5:24). The judicial penalty has been removed. It was paid when Christ was nailed to the cross (see Colossians 2:14).

Imagine yourself in a human court of law. Suppose that you had been arrested for driving under the influence of alcohol and that you had wrecked your car and injured your back. The judge fines you $1,000. He then takes the money out of his own pocket and pays the fine for you. You are free to go. Judicially all has been paid and you do not need to pay a cent. However, because of your sinful actions, your car is still in need of repair and your back still hurts. This is, admittedly, a faulty analogy, but perhaps we can at least get the general idea. The judicial payment for our sin has been paid in full. The Judge paid it Himself. There may be, however, "side effects" which can be costly.

A man listening to the radio heard that a car was headed the wrong way on the highway, forcing people off the road. He realized his wife was on that highway and quickly called her on her cell phone.

"Honey, watch out because a car is going the wrong way and running people off the road!"

She screamed back, "It isn't just one car! There are hundreds of them!"

We can be our own worst enemy. When things are going wrong, perhaps the culprit who is ruining our life is the one we see in the mirror. God may be allowing or even causing us to suffer as a direct and practical result of our sin. We should not expect otherwise. Anyone who abuses drugs or alcohol, whether he is a Christian or not, runs a great risk with his life and health. You might be tempted to think "yes, but *I* would never do that." Maybe our sin is not so obvious, but it may be just as harmful. Our sins may be like little stones which, when piled one on top of the other, eventually come crashing down on us with extensive damage. The law of sowing and reaping has not been overturned.

Sin and its cost to our lives can be very deceiving. Consider how an Eskimo kills a wolf. He first coats his knife blade with blood and allows it to freeze. Then he adds another layer of blood, and then another. As each succeeding smear of blood freezes to the blade of the knife, the Eskimo adds an additional coating until the blade is concealed by a substantial thickness of frozen blood. Then the knife is buried in the frozen ground with the blade up. The marauding wolf follows his sensitive nose to the scent and tastes the fresh frozen blood. He licks it. More and more vigorously the wolf licks the bait until the razor sharp edge is bare. Feverishly now he licks harder. Throughout the arctic night, so great becomes his craving for blood that he does not notice the sting of the naked blade on his own tongue, nor that the blood he is now drinking is his own. His carnivorous appetite craves more and more—until the dawn finds him dead in the snow. We would not set out to ruin our lives or even bring suffering into our lives anymore than the wolf set out to commit suicide. But it can happen and we must be on guard, watching even the small things. As James wrote, "even so the tongue is a little member . . . and defiles the whole body, and sets on fire the course of nature, and it is set on fire by hell" (James 3:5–6).

When the state of Washington first passed a law taxing the retail sale of gasoline, the legislature slipped up on one very important detail: they forgot to attach a penalty to the violation of the law. At first, dealers began collecting and paying the tax, a very small one comparatively, but when they discovered the error in the law, they refused to comply. The legislature then had to be called back into special session in order to attach a penalty to the violation of the tax law. If there was no penalty for not paying income tax, how many would do it? If there was no penalty for stealing, how long would stores remain in business? We need laws and we need penalties to encourage our compliance. God sometimes allows us to suffer the consequences of our sin in order to deter us, warn us, and chastise us for our own good.

The result of sin not only affects our lives, it affects those around us as well. We may be causing others to suffer as a consequence of our sin. A good example of this is an incident in the life of Abraham as recorded in Genesis 20. The situation, in brief, was this: Abraham knew Sarah was beautiful and that others, including nearby King Abimelech, would be willing to kill him in order to get Sarah. Abraham told Sarah to lie about being his wife. Abimelech took Sarah; God threatened Abimelech with death; Abimelech scolded Abraham and returned Sarah. As we look closer at the details of the story, the pervasiveness of sin's effect becomes clear. Indeed, we can see five different levels or groups that sin affects. First, sin affects those we don't even know. According to verses 17–18, "the Lord had closed up all the wombs of the house of Abimelech because of Sarah, Abraham's wife." That list even included servants (v. 17)! Abraham had no intention of harming Abimelech's servants when he lied. You don't mean to harm anyone else, but your sin may touch the lives of people you don't even know.

Second, sin affects those we barely know. It is likely that Abraham and Abimelech would have barely known one another. Abimelech could not have known Abraham well since the lie about Sarah was not immediately apparent. Abimelech was involved and did in fact take Sarah. God's response to Abimelech was, "Indeed you are a dead man because of the woman whom you have taken, for she is a man's wife" (v. 3). Abimelech protested. He maintained (and rightly so!) that he was innocent because he had been lied to (vv. 4–6). Despite his innocence because of ignorance, Abimelech suffered. This is seen by verse 17 which says that "Abraham prayed to God and God healed Abimelech." This was likely an illness which would have resulted in Abimelech's death (see v.7). Further, I believe this illness is what God used to keep Abimelech away from Sarah. In verse 6 God tells Abimelech, "I also withheld you from sinning against Me; therefore I did not let you touch her." In this case, the illness was an evident display of God's grace to Abimelech as well as to Sarah and Abraham. Even so, Abimelech *did* suffer and he was ill because of Abraham's sin. Our sin can affect those we barely know without our even realizing what is going on in their lives or why.

Sin also affects a third group of people: those we know well. Here I am thinking of the effect on Isaac. Isaac was not even born yet but perhaps he grew up hearing the story. It became public knowledge (v. 8), and there are always those who delight in reminding others of their sins. There is an amazing parallel in Genesis 26:6–11. Isaac dwelt in the same place (Gerar), feared the same problem (being killed so others could take his wife), involved a king by the same name (Abimelech—though not necessarily the same person since it was a title like Pharaoh) and resorted to the same lie ("she is my sister"). Where did Isaac learn that? He got it from dad. If you continue in your sin, it is likely your children will too. That does not reduce their guilt; it increases yours. What do your children see concerning your attitude and performance in such areas as prayer, worship, church, service, giving, witnessing, trusting God, responding to trials and responding to temptations? What you do will affect those you care about. Do you want them to pay a price for your actions?

The fourth group is comprised of those who are closest to us. In the case of Abraham in Genesis 20, that would have been Sarah. Abraham placed Sarah in a no-win situation. If she told the truth, she would have to be disobedient to her husband and run the risk of seeing him put to death. If she did not tell the truth, she would, of course, be guilty of lying (which she was, v. 5) and might be taken anyway (which she was, v. 2). Sarah was caught in the middle and she lost. Only the grace and intervention of God spared her worse humiliation and suffering. Our sins will very often affect those who are closest to us. Whether it is something long-term (like an affair) or something short-lived (like blowing up at home because of a problem at work), our spouse and others who are close to us will bear the brunt of our sin.

The last group contains just one person, the individual himself. According to verse 13, Abraham had a continual problem in this area of his life. We know there was at least one other occurrence of similar events (see Genesis 12:10–20). Abraham had predetermined to respond in this way instead of trusting God. Each time he followed his own predetermined course, he failed. It was always also an incident which brought shame upon himself (Genesis 20:8–9) and discredited and dishonored the God he loved and trusted. Abraham caused shame and reproach for himself and multiplied unknown problems for many others. We not only suffer from the practical results of our sins, but we may cause many others to suffer as well. Like a virus, the contamination and damage of sin often spreads from one person to another without notice. We get someone else's virus and another unsuspecting party receives ours. It is not our intention to spread the virus anymore than it is our intention to spread the results of sin; it is simply a natural and tragic consequence to be reckoned with.

Our individual sin may also result in some form of suffering due to our heavenly Father's chastisement. He is faithful to chastise us. We are chastised because He loves us and is concerned about our spiritual growth and development. We must remember that to God our physical and material well-being are important, but our spiritual well-being is more important. Consider the words of Hebrews 12:5–11:

And you have forgotten the exhortation which speaks to you as to sons:
"My son, do not despise the chastening of the Lord,
Nor be discouraged when you are rebuked by Him;
For whom the Lord loves He chastens, And scourges every son whom He receives."
If you endure chastening, God deals with you as with sons; for what son is there whom a father does not chasten?
But if you are without chastening, of which all have become partakers, then you are illegitimate and not sons.
Furthermore, we have had human fathers who corrected us, and we paid them respect. Shall we not much more readily be in subjection to the Father of spirits and live?
For they indeed for a few days chastened us as seemed best to them, but He for our profit, that we may be partakers of His holiness.
Now no chastening seems to be joyful for the present, but painful; nevertheless, afterward it yields the peaceable fruit of righteousness to those who have been trained by it.

Our Father wants the "peaceable fruit of righteousness" to be evident in our lives. For that to happen there will be times when, due to sin, we feel the Father's chastening hand. The chastening may come in various forms. Perhaps for one person it will be the sense of the lack of fellowship with God (1 John 1:6). For another person it may be the loss of material things, especially if they are being placed above God in importance. For yet another person it may be the loss of health. Misusing the Lord's Table (1 Corinthians 11:27–34) is an example of some extreme chastening. The sickness spoken of in James 5:13–20 suggests that sin might be the root of the problem. It is, at any rate, to be considered, and we are told to "confess your trespasses to one another, and pray for one another, that you may be healed" (James 5:16).

The antidote for chastening is confession. "If we confess our sins, He is faithful and just to forgive us our sins and to cleanse us from all unrighteousness" (1 John 1:9). The Father's goal is not to hurt us, but to enable us to grow in Christ, to have fellowship with God and man, and to live a life that is a proper testimony to our gracious Lord.

Before we pass on to another section, it is important to address a relationship of sin and sickness. There are those who maintain that if a person is sick it is because that person has sinned. That may be true. There are, however, other possibilities. When Jesus and his disciples passed by a certain blind man who had been blind from birth, the disciples wanted to know "who sinned, this man or his parents, that he was born blind?" (John 9:2). They were simply voicing a common misconception of their day. To them, the cause of this man's blindness was directly related to personal sin. The only question was *who* had sinned. Jesus' answer set the record straight: "Neither this man nor his parents sinned, but that the works of God should be revealed in him" (John 9:3). Jesus was not saying they were sinless but that the blindness was not related to their sin in any way. We must remember also that Christ suffered, yet He never personally sinned (1 Peter 3:18). We may suffer because of our personal sin, but that does not mean every instance of suffering is related to our sin. I have known men and women who grew closer to God as they aged and yet suffered more. It is not likely that they suffered more because they sinned more. In fact, the opposite appears to be the case; they suffered more, even though they sinned less. The suffering had little or nothing to do with personal sin, but much to do with sin in general (see reason 1) and perhaps other reasons which we shall examine in later chapters.

God is always faithful, even when we are not (2 Timothy 2:13). God does not give up on us. He continues to work in our lives even when we sin, and we can be "confident of this very thing, that He who has begun a good work in you will complete it until the day of Jesus Christ" (Philippians 1:6).

FOR THE PREVENTION OF PRIDE

Pride can lead to painful lessons. When I was first called to preach I spoke with my pastor about it. He offered to let me preach in an evening service two weeks away. I accepted. I already knew what I would preach. I was excited and I was ready. The night of my debut finally came. I preached on "Sharing in God's Victory" and it was a great success. Of all the compliments I received, the best was from my pastor who assured me that God *must* have called me to preach since he had never heard such a good sermon from a beginner and rarely from experienced men. I was puffed up. If I had known about Herod's speech and subsequent death (see Acts 12:20–23!), I would have been trembling in my boots! I once heard Howard Hendricks term the ritual of church folks congratulating their pastor on a sermon "the glorification of the worm!"

Two weeks passed and I was faced with another opportunity to amaze my fortunate audience. There was a problem with the sound system. It kept buzzing and crackling to my dismay. There was a spotlight on me (appropriate, I thought) that developed a short and continually flashed on and off. I dropped my note cards and when I picked them up, I accidentally placed them in the wrong order. I had no idea what I was saying or where I was going. Neither did the unfortunate audience. It was a total disaster in every respect. Still to this day, I often think back on that evening and shudder.

Why did God let me go through that? Had He changed His mind about calling me to be a pastor? Was He not impressed with my first performance? I thought through both messages. What was different outside of the outcome? In the first message, I was dependent upon God; I had prayed and prayed; I had wondered how God could be so gracious to use even someone like me. I had studied the Word and had sought diligently God's guidance as I did. The second time around things were much different but there was one key item that brought about all the change—pride.

God had not changed His mind. He had not given up on me. Because He loved me and still wanted to use me for my good and His glory, He let me suffer the inevitable consequences of my pride. I am thankful that He dealt with that problem so early in my ministry. No, I was not thankful that night. But that was because of a lack of understanding. God was gracious to not let me miss the lesson and He has reinforced it since.

Trials and adversity have a way of waking us up to the realization that we are not as great, self-sufficient, or as "in control" as we thought we were. Our heavenly Father may be using them to prevent pride from entering into us or, when it already has, from taking over our lives. The result of a trial should be character development. The result of pride is destruction. As Proverbs 16:18 puts it: "pride goes before destruction and a haughty spirit before a fall." Now, God does not want us to stumble or fall, and He permits or designs trials and adversity to prevent us from experiencing the ultimate end of pride. Pride cannot lead to loss of salvation, but it can lead to a loss of effective ministry and fellowship with God, which is much more important to God than our temporary comforts.

It would have been a great victory for Satan to have thwarted the ministry of the Apostle Paul. Pride could have done it. The possibilities were great and the opportunity was present. Paul had been greatly used of God and he had been privileged to hear in the third heaven "inexpressible words, which it is not lawful for a man to utter" (2 Corinthians 12:4). Paul could have been exalted by others or by himself, but God sent a lifelong trial to prevent that from happening. Paul's explanation, found in 2 Corinthians 12:7–10, goes like this:

> And lest I should be exalted above measure by the abundance of the revelations, a thorn in the flesh was given to me, a messenger of Satan to buffet me, lest I be exalted above measure.

> Concerning this thing I pleaded with the Lord three times that it might depart from me.

> And He said to me, "My grace is sufficient for you, for My strength is made perfect in weakness." Therefore most gladly I will rather boast in my infirmities, that the power of Christ may rest upon me.

> Therefore I take pleasure in infirmities, in reproaches, in needs, in persecutions, in distresses, for Christ's sake. For when I am weak, then I am strong.

Normally we center our attention in this passage upon the all-sufficiency of God's grace. We are not sure what the thorn was in Paul's life. Perhaps it was purposefully left vague in order that we might be able to plug our own peculiar "thorn" into that passage. What we can be sure of is this—no matter what our affliction may be, God's grace is sufficient for us. Having noted that, though, we do not want miss the *reason* for Paul's thorn. Let's look again at verse 7: "And lest I should be exalted above measure . . . a thorn in the flesh was given to me." God's purpose in this affliction was that Paul would not fall victim to pride. God provided the thorn to prevent the pride and He provided the grace to endure the thorn!

Because of Paul's cryptic description of the thorn as "a messenger of Satan to buffet me" (v. 7), some have wrongly concluded that it was Satan's plan to send the thorn. But Satan is surely not interested in preventing us from being prideful! Indeed, since the garden of Eden (Genesis 3:1–5), Satan has used pride to destroy man. The fall of Lucifer himself is recorded in Isaiah 14:12ff and the root of his problem was pride. No, Satan is not interested in keeping believers from becoming prideful. Why, then, did Paul even mention Satan? This is a demonstration of God's sovereignty, His complete control, over every area. God can use unbelievers as tools to speak to us and even convict us. Do you suppose that Satan is outside of the control of God so that God could not use him? It is ironic, but fitting, that God would use prideful Satan as a tool to prevent pride in Paul's life. Just so in Job's life, we can be assured that Satan was accountable to God and limited in what he could do to Paul.

The problem with pride is not only what it does to us, but what it says about God. Pride says, "I am more important than God." Pride says, "I do not need others *or* God." Pride says, "I deserve this position, favor, promotion, etc., even despite God." Pride robs God of the glory, praise, honor, and credit due Him. David reminds us that God "knows our frame; He remembers that we are dust" (Psalm 103:14). Perhaps we need to capture that thought. A pile of dust is not very valuable. In fact, people get paid to get rid of it. But God took the pile of dust that is you and formed it uniquely together to fashion a human being. To keep that pile of dust from burning in eternal torment, He nailed His Son to a cross. To enable that pile of dust to live a godly life, He places His Holy Spirit within. To use that pile of dust for His glory, He gave gifts and abilities and opportunities. Having achieved some measure of success, how can that pile of dust say, "look at who *I* am and what I've done"? What does that say to God and about God? It robs Him of His glory.

Pride elevates man instead of God. Since that is bad for us and dishonoring to God, adversity may be used to prevent us from falling prey to pride or, having fallen therein, to prevent us from living useless lives in that pit. It is the grace of God that sends the adversity and it is the grace of God that sees us through.

We would do well to heed the instructions of Paul to the Romans (chapter 12, verse 3): "For I say through the grace given to me, to everyone who is among you, not to think of himself more highly than he ought to think, but to think soberly, as God has dealt to each one a measure of faith."

Pride is a faulty mirror. It presents to us an image of ourselves which is untrue. Worse yet, it distorts the image of Christ which we should be reflecting. Adversity can help us get the image right.

TO LEARN GOD'S WAYS

If you have children, you are concerned about the way they live. You are concerned about the way they dress, look, eat, play, study, grow, feel and behave. Where do they learn the *right* way to dress, etc.? Hopefully from you.

Our heavenly Father is even more concerned about the way *we* live. Not just any old way will do! Consider the following passages: "Enter by the narrow gate; for wide is the gate and broad is the way that leads to destruction, and there are many who go in by it. Because narrow is the gate and difficult is the way which leads to life, and there are few who find it" (Matthew 7:13–14). Man is always coming up with alternative "ways," usually in an attempt to be more pleasing to man than God. Proverbs warns that "there is a way that seems right to a man, but its end is the way of death" (14:12). Why settle for second best, especially when the consequences are so drastic? We know that "As for God, His way is perfect" (2 Samuel 22:31). Our goal is not to find *a* way but *the* way. The journey, of course, starts with Jesus who said, "I am the way, the truth, and the life" (John 14:6). Jesus is not only the beginning point of our new life, He *is* our life and our way. As Paul expressed it, "For me to live is Christ, and to die is gain" (Philippians 1:21).

As we travel up the narrow path toward home, we encounter numerous obstacles, detour signs, alternate paths, bright lights on the side of the road and worldly attractions to amuse, entertain and detract us from the Way.

What happens when we go astray? Our Father teaches us the right way. Sometimes that lesson can be learned only through the crucible of affliction.

David was a man after God's own heart. He was greatly used of God but he was not perfect. There were times when David went astray and found himself not walking in God's way. God did not give up on David. Instead, His loving hand formed a perfect affliction to bring David back into the way everlasting. David recognized it afterwards and he wrote, "Before I was afflicted I went astray, but now I keep your word . . . It is good for me that I have been afflicted, that I may learn your statutes" (Psalm 119:67, 71).

All of Psalm 119 concerns the Word of God. It is variously expressed by the designations of God's commandments, statutes, precepts, truth, testimonies, law, judgments, ordinances, words and ways. Every one of the 176 verses contains one or more of those terms or ideas. They are synonyms with various shades of meaning and they all center around God's Word and God's way. David found that to walk in God's way required an intimate knowledge of God's Word. Even the first verse of this Psalm says "Blessed are the undefiled in the way, who walk in the law of the Lord!" David's heart desire was "Oh, that my ways were directed to keep your statues!" (v. 5). To David's question "How can a young man cleanse his way?" He answers, "By taking heed according to Your word" (v. 9). Many are the verses that speak of God's way and all of them are linked to God's Word.

Going back now to Psalm 119:67, we see that David admits the error of his way ("I went astray") and has found the remedy ("but now I keep Your word"). But what was it that brought this to David's mind? God used affliction as the schoolmaster. As David said, "*Before* I was afflicted I went astray . . ." No affliction seems good at the time, but David, later realizing God's purpose in it, was able to say: "It is good for me that I have been afflicted, that I may learn your statutes" (Psalm 119:71).

Suffering can drive us to God and cause us to learn more of His ways. To enumerate God's ways would be far beyond the scope of this chapter and even of this book. However, for simplicity's sake we can examine one area which encompasses many of the others. It is helpful to ask, "What are God's priorities for my life?"

It would be amusing if it were not so distressful to see what others consider God's priorities to be. Some believe that God's priorities are need related (i.e., the "health and wealth gospel"). Others believe that God's main goal is to get us to just love one another—even if we worship different gods. Others believe that God's priorities center around how we dress, cut our hair and conform to some external (and often legalistic) model. What is most important, however, is what God says.

God's priority for every believer is the same. It is expressed in many places and in different forms but it always comes down to one item. God's ultimate priority for our lives is perhaps most clearly expressed by Romans 8:29: "For whom He foreknew, He also predestined to be conformed to the image of His Son, that He might be the firstborn among many brethren." Being the image of Christ, or being Christlike, is God's top priority for every believer. To the point that a believer is Christlike, he is walking in God's ways. To deviate from Christlikeness is to abandon God's ways. We can therefore safely say that to learn God's ways is to learn Christlikeness and to follow God's ways is to follow Christ. He is our pattern and He is the Father's top priority for our lives. We are to know Him, love Him, trust Him, obey Him, and live like Him.

I once worked in the quality control section of a factory that produced two-way radios. My job was to test the finished radio to see if it measured up to a predetermined standard. I could not change the standard or accept inferior quality. If the radio did not measure up to the standard in every single area, it went back to be repaired. The radio went back and forth as many times as it took to make it measure up to the standard. God has set before us the standard of His Son. Until we reach that standard He will continue to work in us (Philippians 1:6). Likewise, we must continue to work toward that standard "till we all come to the unity of the faith and the knowledge of the Son of God, to a perfect man, to the measure of the stature of the fullness of Christ" (Ephesians 4:13). Although that standard will not be attained by any of us this side of heaven, God does not lower His standard. Of primary importance is our direction and our progress. Our lives must be heading toward Christlikeness. In those areas where we are not making progress we need to learn God's ways. He may choose to get our attention and to teach us through adversity. His quality control is perfect!

God's grace and mercy and patience are demonstrated to us by the fact that even though we fail to measure up to His ways every day, we are not afflicted every day. He gives us time to grow and to learn. We do not expect three-year-olds to run a marathon, but we do expect them to walk on their own. We expect to see progress but we realize it takes time. Our Father expects us to be in the process of learning His ways.

The lessons do not always come through adversity. God may use a sermon, a book, a radio program, a Bible passage encountered during devotions, a testimony, a hymn, or a number of other means to speak to our hearts. One of those possible means is, of course, adversity. If that is the case with us, might we be able to say with David, "It is good for me that I have been afflicted, that I might learn from your statutes."

Like sheep, we need direction from the Great Shepherd. We know that, "all we like sheep have gone astray; we have turned, every one, to his own way; and the Lord has laid on Him the iniquity of us all" (Isaiah 53:6). He has not only made provision for our salvation, but also for our daily walk. To the Jews in captivity who may have been wondering if God had completely given up on them, Isaiah wrote the following words:

> And though the Lord gives you the bread of adversity and the water of affliction, yet your teachers will not be moved in a corner anymore, but your eyes shall be your teachers, Your ears shall hear a word behind you saying, This is the way, walk in it.
>
> (Isaiah 30:20–21)

May the Lord give us the grace to learn and to walk in all His way.

TO LEARN PATIENCE

When I was the pastor of a church in Texas, I attended an all-day conference for ministers. One of the main speakers related rather sheepishly the following story. He was running late because his alarm had failed to ring. In his haste to make up for lost time he cut himself shaving. Then he found that his shirt was not ironed. To make matters worse, running to his car he noticed a tire was flat. Disgusted, and by this time thoroughly distraught, this pastor finally got underway with a sudden burst of speed. Racing through town he failed to notice a stop sign and rushed through it. It so happened that there was a policeman nearby, and the man soon heard the scream of a siren. Jumping out of his car, the agitated minister said sharply, "Well, go ahead and give me a ticket. Everything else has gone wrong today!" The policeman walked up and said quietly, "Sir, I used to have days like that before I became a Christian." What a humbling experience! We should notice at least two lessons from this story: (1) we are all susceptible to lack of patience, and (2) as Christians we all have the capacity for patience.

We all want patience. Our problem is that we want it right now and we want it for free. We don't want to wait and we don't want to pay and as a result we don't learn patience. There are two necessary ingredients to arrive at patience: time and trials.

Time is a slow but meticulous teacher. "The years teach much which the days never know," wrote Emerson. We give up too easily and too soon. During its first year the Coca Cola Company sold only 400 cokes. Dr. Seuss's first children's book was rejected by 23 publishers. The 24th publisher sold 6 million copies. During his first three years in the automobile business, Henry Ford went bankrupt twice. We all admire a tall, sturdy and beautiful oak tree but we may fail to realize that it took many years and the survival of many storms to attain its majestic and honored status. We want our Christian lives to be like that oak, but we have patience enough only to become a watermelon. We cannot circumvent time.

To move successfully through both time and trials requires trust. The Lord indicates this truth by His repeated use of the word "wait." We are not simply told to wait but we are told specifically to "wait on the Lord." For instance, Psalm 27:14 says, "Wait on the Lord; be of good courage, and He shall strengthen your heart; wait, I say, on the Lord!"

Our problem is not waiting for the Lord's provision as much as waiting for the Lord's timing. It is not that the Lord has not yet provided what we need, but that we do not use what He has already provided (2 Peter 1:3–4; Romans 8:32). Waiting on the Lord refers to waiting for His timing. The reason we must wait for His timing is because of all the unseen factors involved. God, being not only all-knowing but completely sovereign, has perfect timing. Since His ways are far above our ways (Isaiah 55:8–9), we must gladly submit to His timetable. When I see youngsters crashing their bikes, I am reminded of the wisdom of setting a time limit (minimum age) for a driver's license, even at the risk of causing teens to be impatient. Timing may save their lives and others. When I see a cake rising in the oven, I know better than to eat it before the chef claims it is finished. It has to be in the fire long enough to be completed, and so do we.

That which we cannot see behind God's timing is exactly that which makes it so crucial to wait. Some related factors are God's working in events, history, and other people's lives; God's eternal and unchangeable plan—the timing of which only He has set and knows (Acts 1:7), and God's leading and development in our own lives. All these factors and others come into play and only God, Who sees the whole picture and declares the end from the beginning, is capable of knowing the right timing.

You may be suffering and wondering why God has not yet intervened. If it were up to you the suffering would have ended long ago! But perhaps now it is even worse! Has God forgotten you, abandoned you, or messed up on His timing? No! Likely, that was what the Jews thought under the cruel taskmasters of Egypt. After many years of suffering as slaves to Pharaoh, God sent Moses. Moses went to Pharaoh to ask for the freedom of the Israelites to go into the wilderness and offer sacrifices. Pharaoh declined. Instead, he increased their work load. "Thanks a lot, Moses!" might express the Israelites' response. Moses brings before God the following question: "Lord, why have You brought trouble on this people? Why is it You sent me? For since I came to Pharaoh to speak in Your name, he has done evil to this people; neither have You delivered Your people at all" (Exodus 5:22–23). God's grace is evident in that the next verse does not read "and so Moses died from a terrible plague!" Moses was asking the question which sometimes creeps into our hearts, "Lord, why haven't You yet delivered me?" It is questioning God's timing. From our perspective, knowing how the story turns out, we might want to console Moses and the Israelites with "don't worry, God has everything under control." Perhaps we need to say that to ourselves! God's purpose for not delivering them so soon and so easily is expressed in Exodus 6:6–7. In short, God wanted them to know that it was He and He alone Who had delivered them. If they had been let go at the first request, they would not have seen the mighty hand of God and may have felt indebted more to Pharaoh than to God for their release. God has a purpose in all that happens to us. It is not important to see that purpose now. It is important to trust God in everything—even in the timing.

Keith missed flight 139. A number of frustrating events had delayed him and now the plane which was to carry him to a vital meeting in Los Angeles had departed without him. "How could God allow this to happen? I *needed* to get to that meeting. I thought God met my needs!" Questions and confusion and disappointment reigned in Keith's heart. Then he heard the news—flight 139 never made it to L.A. God's timing is perfect, even if we do not so clearly and quickly get the message the way Keith did.

It is not time alone that teaches patience. Time has as its cohort and companion trials. James speaks directly to the issue when he writes: "My brethren, count it all joy when you fall into various trials" (James 1:2). Working through the verse we find a number of significant facts. First, James addresses them as "my brethren," indicating they were believers. We should not think it strange that as Christians we are put through trials (see also 1 Peter 4:12 and John 16:33). Secondly, when the trials do come we are to "count it all joy." Notice that James is not saying it *is* joyful but that despite our dislike of it we are to "count it all joy." In order to do that we must remember that God has a purpose and that He is in control. It was not a joyful experience for the apostles to be shamefully treated by the Sanhedrin, yet we read that "they departed from the presence of the council, rejoicing that they were counted worthy to suffer shame for His name" (Acts 5:41). Thirdly, experiencing trials is not a question of "if" but "when." As James says, ". . . when you fall into various trials." Fourth, James calls them "various trials." Not all trials are the same in depth, length, or kind.

One of God's expressed purposes in trials is given in verse 3: "knowing that the testing of your faith produces patience." Paul stated in similar terms, ". . . we also glory in tribulations, knowing that tribulation produces perseverance" (Romans 5:3). What is the connection between trials and patience? God's provision. Anxiety is the opposite of patience. Anxiety shows that we are uncertain of God's hand. He never fails. He always provides. As I look back over a great number of trials I realize that God never let me down. In most cases He put me to shame by even providing more than what I needed to get through. His grace has always been in abundance, His mercy never lacking. As I go through a trial now, I can see much more patience. Anxiety looks at self and says, "I can't!" whereas patience looks to God and says "God can!"

James goes on to say, "But let patience have its perfect work, that you may be perfect and complete, lacking nothing" (James 1:4). A key word here is "let." We are to cooperate with, not fight against, all that God is trying to do. To cooperate will mean learning the lesson as it was intended the first time. To not cooperate will mean repeating the lesson.

Since patience is directly related to trust, it is an important lesson for us to learn. God is not honored by a lack of trust in our lives. He will send not only trials but will provide all we need to come through victoriously in order that we might learn to trust Him and thereby learn patience.

TO LEARN TO COMFORT OTHERS

John was numb with shock as he stared at the hospital door behind which lay the lifeless form of his infant son. A friend from church walked up to him, smiled and quoted "All things work together for good . . ." John confessed to me later that he felt like punching his "friend" but somehow managed to control himself. It was a case of the right words at the wrong time.

Brenda needed a word encouragement and hope and comfort. Even though she was a relatively young woman, she had just gone through a hysterectomy. A grandmother from her church came by and reassured her that there was really nothing to it and that she herself had the same operation. It was a case of the right time but the wrong words.

True words of comfort are precious. Blessed is that one who knows how and when to use them. I have learned that when the Lord has not given me anything helpful to say, I (and the potential hearers!) profit most by my saying nothing. Sometimes we can be of best use just by being present, just by a silent demonstration of our concern.

Youfei Thomas was one of my African students while I was a missionary in the Central African Republic. Actually, I believe Thomas taught me more than I taught him. One day he walked to my house and asked if I would like to go with him to the local dispensary. I agreed to go but I was not sure why we were going.

"Are you sick, Thomas?"

No, I am well. My wife is sick."

I knew his wife, Marie, was pregnant. Now I learned that she also had parasites as well as malaria. She was sixteen.

"How can I help you, Thomas? Do you want me to help you carry her?"

"No, that is not necessary."

"Do you want me to pray?"

"Yes, but you could do that in your home as well. That is not why I asked you to come."

Marie met us at the door. She was burning up with fever, her eyes were glazed over and she was very weak. Still, she greeted us with a smile and then began walking, slowly and unassisted (as per their culture) toward the dispensary. It took awhile to make the journey and I had time to think on the way. It finally dawned on me why I was needed. This very poor family had no way to pay for the medical services or drugs.

"Thomas, you have helped me much since I have come here. Let me pay for this medical attention for you."

"No," Thomas said in an even voice, "I did not ask you to come so that you could pay my bill."

We finally arrived at the dispensary. It was teeming with men, women, and children suffering from a wide variety of ailments. We all waited outside, sitting on logs and shaded from the intense sun by a typical thatched roof. As I sat with Thomas, I noticed that others passing by would usually stop and talk with one or more of those waiting. After awhile they would get up and continue their journey.

Marie was finally seen, treated with what little they could do, given medicine and released. Still being unsure of why I was needed, and being a little dense, I asked Thomas as we walked why he had needed me.

"It is our custom that when someone is ill or in trouble or in grief we spend time with them. We do not have to *do* anything. We do not have to *give* anything. We show our concern by being with them. When they weep, we weep and when they laugh, we laugh."

Somehow it all sounded biblical. I was convicted to the core. My friend and teacher, Thomas, simply smiled at me as I left for home. I sensed that I was walking out of a classroom.

Many people have misconceptions about what it means to comfort others. Perhaps we tend to be more like Job's "comforters" instead of like the Comforter Jesus spoke of (John 16). The "comfort passage" (2 Corinthians 1:3–4) is often either misunderstood or misapplied. Numerous times I have heard people use this passage to say: "God allowed me to go through this trial, divorce, illness, etc., so that I could identify with others in the same circumstance and talk with them as one who 'knows' and be of some help to them." Let me say that this is a very noble intention. Further, it would be pleasing to our Lord to see that His children desired to minister to one another in such a way. However, that is not what this passage is teaching us to do. In fact, if what we point people to is our parallel circumstance and how we made it though, we may miss a chance to point others to God and to glorify Him. Too often it is our doctor, lawyer, or counselor who gets the praise.

It is true that God may allow us to go through some adversity in order that we can be a comfort to others. The question is, "In what way can I be a comforter?" It is not only to those I can directly identify with. What would we then say to those suffering with something we haven't experienced yet? "Sorry, I haven't gone through that yet. Find someone else!" I will never be able to identify with a woman in childbirth. Even if circumstances seem parallel (two women, for example, who had both had a hysterectomy), there may be other additional factors (one a grandmother but the other with no children) which make the comparison hardly equal. That is not to say that a hysterectomy is easy for the grandmother, but other factors enter in to make the situation somewhat different.

A closer look at Second Corinthians will help us to see how we can be a comfort to others, whether we have gone through a like experience or not. The passage reads:

> Blessed be the God and Father of our Lord Jesus Christ, the Father of mercies and God of all comfort, who comforts us in all our tribulation, that we may be able to comfort those who are in any trouble, with the comfort with which we ourselves are comforted by God.
>
> (2 Corinthians 3:4)

There are five points to consider if we are to have a clear picture of what this passage is saying. They are:

1. *God* is the God of all comfort. It is *He* who comforts us and not someone else, not another's circumstance or parallel experience. "Blessed be the God . . ." means He is to be praised. It is okay to say "I had that operation and Dr. Doe did a fine job." But that is not biblical comfort! What that person needs to know is that even if Dr. Doe blows it, God is there and He never, never fails.

2. God comforts us *in* all our tribulation. We are always looking for the quickest and easiest way out. Our hope is not based on the fact that we will soon be out of this problem (which may not be true) but rather that every step of the way God is with us. When Paul asked "What shall separate us from the love of Christ?" (Romans 8:35), he listed a number of potential dangers and then concluded, "Yet in all these things we are more than conquerors through Him who loved us" (Romans 8:37). Note and underline that word "in." We are not to comfort others with "someday you will be out of this" but rather with God's grace is sufficient *in* this time. He will not leave you or forsake you. Nothing can separate you from the love of God which is in Christ Jesus our Lord."

3. God comforts us in *all* our tribulation. He does not mean for us to be comforted in only these areas in which someone else can identify with us. God Himself knows perfectly well our every need and hurt. He keeps track of every tear (Psalm 56:8). When no other person understands, God does. We are His precious children and He is our caring Father. Our comfort comes from God and it comes "in all our tribulation."

4. God comforts us for a specific purpose. He expresses that by the purpose clause in verse four: "that we may be able to comfort those who are in any trouble." God does not intend for us simply to be comforted and then go back to life as usual. We are to use that comfort to bless others and glorify God. Notice that we are to do this, not just to those in like circumstances, but to "those

50

who are in *any* trouble." This is the crucial point. Our common denominator is not the problem we went through, but God. We are not to point others to our problems or our successes. We are to point them to God.

5. The comfort we are to give is the same as that which we ourselves received. This is expressed by the end of verse four which says ". . . with the comfort with which we ourselves are comforted by God." When we ask, "what comfort is that?" we are brought back to verse three and the beginning of verse four. We come back full circle to the first three points above. Our goal is not that *we* would be their comfort, but that they would be "comforted by God." It is that which will bring them the most hope and comfort. It is that which will bring God the most glory. Comfort is not found unless there is hope; hope is not found unless there is God.

Perhaps God has enabled you to have victory in some adversity and to experience His peace in the storm and His comfort in the pain. Point others to Him that they might also know "the comfort with which we ourselves are comforted by God."

Even if you have not gone through the adversity, you can still point others to God. God has also supplied you with ready examples of His great grace and working in lives. He recorded numerous such examples in His Word. As Paul wrote in another place: "For whatever things were written before were written for our learning, that we through the patience and comfort of the Scriptures might have hope" (Romans 15:4).

We could end this thought no better than with what God has already done through His servant Paul, namely:

Now may the God of patience and comfort grant you to be likeminded toward one another, according to Christ Jesus, that you may with one mind and one mouth glorify the God and Father of our Lord Jesus Christ.

(Romans 15:5–6)

THAT GOD MIGHT BE GLORIFIED

Fruity people glorify God. That is why Jesus said: "By this My Father is glorified, that you bear much fruit . . ." (John 15:8). What kind of fruit was He referring to? The fruit that comes from a life in harmony with the vine. This fruit is named specifically for us in Galatians 5:22 and 23 as: ". . . love, joy, peace, longsuffering, kindness, goodness, faithfulness, gentleness, self-control . . . "

The pruning process (John 15:2) is designed to enable us to produce more fruit. This process may very well involve some sort of adversity since a primary lesson is that of our need to abide in Christ—without which there is no fruit (John 15:4). Indeed, we can do nothing without Him (John 15:5).

Even an unbeliever can have some semblance of love, joy, peace, etc., when things are going well. But when adversity comes, it's another story. It is during such times, when a believer clings to the Vine and draws his strength from that relationship, that his light shines and the Father is glorified. Countless are the testimonies of those who have had peace in the storm and joy in the trial. They have learned and demonstrated that the fruit of the Spirit is not dependent upon external conditions, but internal conditions.

God expects us to depend upon Him for grace and strength and enablement to know and display the fruit of the Spirit in times of adversity.

In Psalm 50, verse 15, God says: "Call upon Me in the day of trouble; I will deliver you, and you shall glorify Me." He invites us to call on Him and He promises to deliver us—which is our primary concern. But God has a deeper purpose: ". . . and you shall glorify me."

The idea of God's glory is an often repeated theme in Scripture. It finds its expression in a number of texts and situations (such as 1 Cor. 10:31; 1 Peter 2:12; Rev. 4:11; Ps. 24:8; etc.). God does nothing without purpose and the highest purpose is His own glory. But what does "glory" mean and how do we "glorify" God? The following description by Gary Inrig is helpful:[3]

> The Greek word for glory originally described someone's opinion ("what I think") and also came to mean one's reputation ("what others think of me"). In this sense, an individual's glory is his fame and honor. Thus the Lord Jesus says to the Jewish leaders, "I do not accept praise (glory) from men. How can you believe if you receive praise (glory) from one another, yet make no effort to obtain the praise (glory) that comes from the only God?" (John 5:41, 44 NIV). One's glory is one's reputation. But in the New Testament, "glory" also points to the substance which stands behind the praise. God's glory is not just His reputation, but His revealed character, the display of His attributes. To glorify someone therefore is to increase his reputation by revealing his true nature.

A believer can and should do that in everyday life, but the time of adversity will be the real test. To respond like an unbeliever, "as others who have no hope" (1 Thess. 4:13), does not help our situation or, more importantly, bring glory to God. Conversely, to respond by faith and cast our cares upon Him (1 Peter 5:7) glorifies God. If our situation improves, we have further opportunity to increase God's reputation by telling others of God's grace and working in our lives. If our situation does not improve, we still have opportunity to reveal God's true nature in and through our lives.

Diane has terminal cancer. According to the doctors, she should have departed this life months ago. Whenever I see her, she always asks the same prayer request—that she might be a testimony for God to the very end. She tells whoever crosses her path that God has enabled her to continue on and that He is her source of strength. She has been a testimony to believers and unbelievers alike; she has laid up treasures in heaven and she has glorified God on earth.

The connection of adversity and God's glory is clearly demonstrated in two passages found in the Gospel of John.

The first passage (John 9) tells of a man who was blind from birth. Jesus explained to His disciples, in response to their question, that the reason the man was blind was not because of his sin or his parents' sin, ". . . but that the works of God should be revealed in him" (John 9:3). In other words, God would be glorified because of the works Christ (an indication of His deity—vv. 3–4) was about to do.

Christ did heal the man and display the power of God. That it was a notable miracle is indicated by verse 32: "since the world began it has been unheard of that anyone opened the eyes of one who was born blind."

There is a touch of irony in verse 24. The Pharisees insisted that the man quit talking about Jesus as the healer and "give God the glory!" Jesus called them blind (39–41) because they could not see that the glory *was* going to God. Spiritual blindness is worse than physical blindness.

We may tend to feel sorry for this man who was born blind "just so Jesus could perform a miracle." But that man knew the hand of God on him in a very special way. He had his eyes opened—not just physically, but spiritually—and he has been enjoying the scenery of heaven for a couple thousand years. Weep instead for those who are spiritually blind!

Lazarus encountered some adversity. In fact, he died from it. Why? It was for the glory of God.

John, chapter eleven, contains the account of the death and resurrection of Lazarus. When Jesus was told that Lazarus was sick, He replied, "this sickness is not unto death" (John 11:4). Jesus did not make a mistake or misjudge the gravity of the situation. He knew how the story was going to turn out. By the end of the chapter Lazarus is *not* dead and Jesus' words are vindicated.

The *purpose* of Lazarus' problem was not his death "but for the glory of God, that the Son of God may be glorified through it" (John 11:4). This is an indication of the deity of Christ since to glorify the Son of

God means to glorify God. But the main point here is that Jesus, at the very beginning, points out God's divine purpose in the events to follow, namely, His glory.

If Jesus had been present with Lazarus at the time of his illness and had simply healed him, that would have certainly been a miracle, but then we would not have the tremendous story and words of comfort and demonstration of power which are ours in this passage. It is good that Lazarus died. Jesus, we are told, "said to them plainly, Lazarus is dead. And I am glad for your sakes that I was not there, that you may believe . . ." (John 11:14–15). If Jesus had asked Martha and Mary whether they considered it "good" that Lazarus had died, I am sure they would have answered "no." The higher purpose, which they could not see through their grief-stricken eyes was the glory of God. The question of how God might be glorified through their trial was over-shadowed by the question of "Why weren't you here in time?" The answer is that Jesus was there at the exact right time to accomplish His twofold purpose: the resurrection of Lazarus and the glorification of God.

Later, when Jesus had come to the grave, He commanded that the stone be rolled away. Martha reminded Jesus that Lazarus had been dead for several days. The Lord replied to her: "Did I not say to you that if you would believe you would see the glory of God?" (John 11:40). The Lord will be glorified whether we believe or not. If you, however, want to *see* the glory of God, you must believe (John 9:39–41; 11:42).

The display of the glory of God also leads to belief. Immediately following the raising and loosing of Lazarus we read: "Then many of the Jews who had come to Mary, and had seen the things Jesus did, believed in Him" (John 11:45). In fact, so many people began to believe in Jesus because of this live and notable testimony that the chief priests wanted to kill Lazarus as well as Jesus (John 12:10–11).

The supreme example of suffering leading to God's glory is Jesus Himself. Jesus, looking toward the cross in His near future, told His followers: "The hour has come that the Son of Man should be glorified" (John 12:23).

We think of the cross of Christ as being for us. It is true that on the cross our Lord paid for our sins, but that is not the whole story. The cross brought glory to the Son and it brought glory to the Father. There was no other road to glory than the one that led up Calvary's hill. God may also be giving you the privilege of bringing glory to Him through your affliction.

If you had to choose between being released from suffering and glorifying God, which would you choose? We are all glad that Jesus chose to glorify God through suffering. Part of His struggle over this question is recorded for us in John 12:27: "Now My soul is troubled, and what shall I say? 'Father, save me from this hour'? But for this purpose I came to this hour. Father, glorify Your name."

If you are undergoing suffering right now, could you say "Father, glorify Your name?" For God to do that might mean increased suffering on your part so that He might display His power to others through your life. It might also mean that God would intervene on your behalf with a supernatural deliverance so that He might display His power to others by what He has accomplished in your life. We, of course, would rather have the second solution, but are we willing to say, "Father glorify Your name, no matter what?"

Let us remember the words given through the apostle Peter: "beloved, do not think it strange concerning the fiery trial which is to try you, as though some strange thing happened to you; but rejoice to the extent that you partake of Christ's sufferings, that when His glory is revealed, you may also be glad with exceeding joy" (1 Peter 4:12–13).

God, speaking to Israel in their rejection through the prophet Isaiah, promised an end to their chastisement and a restoration to the land. He would not forget His own. He would restore "Everyone who is called by My name, whom I have created for My glory . . ." (Isaiah 43:7).

BECAUSE OF DEMONIC ACTIVITY

One of the most alarming verses in Scripture is 1 Peter 5:8, where Peter warns: "Be sober, be vigilant, because your adversary the devil walks about like a roaring lion, seeking whom he may devour." Not a comforting thought!

I have often been asked if a believer can be possessed by a demon, and to what degree Satan can influence and disrupt our life, health, and spiritual well-being. The answer is not easy to come by.

Most of the material concerning demon possession or demonic influence has to do with unbelievers. This is true both of the accounts in the Bible as well as more modern times. Perhaps this in itself should tell us something.

In my years in the ministry, both as a pastor and as a missionary in Africa, I have seldom come across anyone that I thought to be demon possessed. I have *never* known a believer to be demon possessed. There is not a case in the Bible where a believer was possessed by a demon and it seems biblically and theologically improbable if not impossible. Not only do we belong to God as His precious possession, but we are filled with His Holy Spirit. Our body has become the temple (holy of holies!) of the Holy Spirit (1 Cor. 6:19). It does not seem likely that a demon would be welcome there or feel comfortable there for any amount of time!

There are those (usually foreign missionaries to isolated areas) who can from their personal experience recount tales of believers being demon possessed.[4] It is a dangerous thing, however, to build theology around experiences. Perhaps much of the problem hinges on terminology. Demonic activity and influence, which *can* be evident even in a believer's life, may have been mistaken for possession.

Three separate cases of demonic activity/influence as found in the Bible will be briefly examined. They are Job, Ananias and his wife Sapphira, and the Apostle Paul.

Job, of course, contains the most detailed account in Scripture of Satan's attack on one of God's people. It would be good to study the whole book in order to appreciate its full significance, and the reader is urged to do so, but the scope of this chapter will only permit us some pointed considerations.

It must be noted that Job was not open to Satan's attack *because* he was a sinful man. Job was a sinner (a fact he had to come to grips with) but the author is careful to point out at the outset that Job was "blameless and upright, and one who feared God and shunned evil" (Job 1:1). Most of us would relish such a testimony about ourselves! Just because someone experiences demonic and/or Satanic activity does not indicate he is more sinful than most believers. It seems more likely that Satan would seek to destroy the testimony of someone who is doing right than someone who is destroying their own testimony without his help.

One of the most significant features in the story of Job is the exchange between Satan and God. Satan is seen as having to give an account of his activities (1:7; 2:2). This is not because God was uninformed and needed a news update but rather for the purpose it has served over the centuries—to demonstrate Satan's accountability. Satan is also withheld from doing anything more than what God expressly permits (1:12; 2:6). Even though Satan or his demons can inflict great harm in the life of a believer, nothing—mark that, *nothing*—can come into your life without first passing through the hands of your heavenly Father. We are never in Satan's hands; we are always in the Father's hands (John 10:28–30).

If the terrible events in Job's life had fallen on one of lesser faith and devotion (such as us?), the outcome might have been failure instead of victory. The point is, it didn't! God allowed this degree of Satan's activity in Job's life because He knew Job's mettle and that it would be purified but not consumed in this fiery trial.

It appears that even when God does allow Satan's involvement in the life of a believer, the outcome is always positive for those who keep their trust in God. That is not to say that Job had a pleasant experience! Job did, however, gain from the experience. He knew God and himself better, as expressed in 42:5–6: "I have heard of You by the hearing of the ear, but now my eyes see You. Therefore I abhor myself and repent in dust and ashes." The Lord compensated Job for his losses (though He was not obligated to do so) in that He "gave Job twice as much as he had before" (Job 42:10). Even Job's "friends" learned firsthand of Job's vindication by God (42:7–9). Overall, Job gained socially, materially, and most importantly, spiritually through this experience. God never fails the soul that trusts in Him.

Paul's problem with the thorn in his flesh and Satan's involvement has already been discussed (see the reason "The Prevention of Pride"), and we will just note it briefly here.

Paul's description, as found in 2 Corinthians 12:7–10, does seem to attribute a role to Satan. However, we must keep in mind the following details: (1) Paul was *not* possessed; (2) God sent the "thorn" to protect Paul from pride; (3) God supplied sufficient grace for His servant Paul; (4) God used the situation to display His strength in Paul's weakness; (5) Paul learned from the situation (vv. 9–10); (6) Paul was still able to have a lengthy and effective ministry (to say the least) despite the thorn and perhaps, in some ways, *because* of the thorn; and (7) we and thousands of other believers have gained strength and comfort and understanding from Paul's suffering. I am glad we have this passage. I am not glad that Paul had to suffer, but given the choice of his suffering versus the benefits received, I would choose his suffering. It is obvious that I am on God's side in this since God, Who reigns over all, saw fit to send the thorn. Even Paul, though not enjoying the suffering, was able to say, "Therefore most gladly I will rather boast in my infirmities, that the power of Christ may rest upon me" (2 Corinthians 12:9).

Satan may have had a hand (by God's permission) in Paul's suffering, but because of Paul's relationship with the Lord and because of his trust in God, the outcome was positive. God never fails the soul that trusts in Him.

Job and Paul are glorious and notable demonstrations of the power of God despite Satan's attack. The outcome has not always been so glorious, sad to say. The problem, of course, is not the waning of God's power but rather the lack of faithfulness on the part of people. Paul wrote to Timothy: "If we are faithless, he remains faithful; He cannot deny Himself" (2 Timothy 2:13). Later in the same chapter Paul instructs that a servant of the Lord must teach earnestly and humbly those who are in opposition "that they may come to their senses and escape the snare of the devil, having been taken captive by him to do his will" (2 Timothy 2:26).

When we come to the story of Ananias and Sapphira we should marvel not that they died, but rather that we live. Acts chapter 5 is a black spot on the early pages of Church history. Especially after the glowing reports of the last half of Acts 4, Acts 5:1–11 is a dark day indeed. Unfortunately, the Church today resembles the first part of Acts 5 more than it does the last part of Acts 4!

The biblical account of the incident reads as follows:

But a certain man named Ananias, with Sapphira his wife, sold a possession.

And he kept back part of the proceeds, his wife also being aware of it, and brought a certain part and laid it at the apostles' feet.

But Peter said, "Ananias, why has Satan filled your heart to lie to the Holy Spirit and keep back part of the price of the land for yourself? While it remained, was it not your own? And after it was sold, was it not in your own control? Why have you conceived this thing in your heart? You have not lied to men but to God."

Then Ananias, hearing these words, fell down and breathed his last. So great fear came upon all those who heard these things.

And the young men arose and wrapped him up, carried him out, and buried him.

Now it was about three hours later when his wife came in, not knowing what had happened.

And Peter answered her, "Tell me whether you sold the land for so much?" And she said, "Yes, for so much."

Then Peter said to her, "How is it that you have agreed together to test the Spirit of the Lord? Look, the feet of those who have buried your husband are at the door, and they will carry you out."

Then immediately she fell down at his feet and breathed her last. And the young men came in and found her dead, and carrying her out, buried her by her husband.

So great fear came upon all the church and upon all who heard these things.

There is a question as to whether or not Ananias and Sapphira were genuine believers. It does no good to say that by their sin they showed themselves to be nonbelievers, for in that case the Church would be made up of only one Person! Dr. Homer Kent lists four factors which indicate they were probably genuine Christians. As he writes, it does seem preferable to view Ananias and Sapphira as believers who were disciplined by God for the following reasons:[5]

> (1) Acts 4:32 indicates that all who engaged in the community of goods were believers, and though Ananias and Sapphira are contrasted with Barnabas, there is nothing to indicate that they were not understood as members of the "multitude of them that believed." (2) Satan can energize saved people (David, 1 Chron. 21:1; Peter, Matt. 16:21–23; Christians in general, 1 Peter 5:8, 9). (3) Physical death is a discipline applied to some Christians (1 Cor. 11:30–32). (4) The fact of lying to the Holy Spirit is more easily understood of Christians indwelt by the Spirit than of unbelievers who have no relation to God and certainly have no special relationship to the Holy Spirit.

If it is true that they were believers, we are faced with the problem of explaining Satan's activity. Peter directly asks Ananias: ". . . why has Satan filled your heart to lie to the Holy Spirit . . ." (Acts 5:3). It is interesting to note that Peter was the very one to whom Jesus had earlier turned and said "Get behind Me, Satan! You are an offense to Me, for you are not mindful of the things of God, but the things of men" (Matt. 16:23). Now Jesus did not mean that Peter had turned into Satan but that Peter was, like Satan, working against God's will and had become a mouthpiece for Satan.[6]

Peter was probably referring to a similar problem on the part of Ananias and Sapphira. They had been influenced by Satan (the father of lies—John 8:44) to lie to God.

It is important to note that it was not Peter who caused their death. He may have been as surprised by it as anyone there. Peter just asked the question and "then Ananias, hearing these words, fell down and breathed his last" (Acts 5:5). Three hours later a similar fate fell upon Sapphira.

What was the difference between Job and Paul and this couple? Job and Paul were able to say: "All I have and am belongs to God" and mean it. Ananias and Sapphira tried to say the same thing but they did not mean it. To them, material blessings and physical comforts meant more than righteousness before God. The Lord had not demanded that they give *anything* (Acts 5:4). The problem was not that they didn't give enough, but that they lied about what they did give, and by so doing attempted to bring praise upon themselves instead of God. Satan attacked the spiritual life of all four of these through their physical life. With Job and Paul he was unsuccessful. With Ananias and Sapphira, Satan won and they lost. The difference was trust and devotion.

There is a fable of a skylark who came from a noble skylark family. He loved to fly high above the earth and sing beautiful melodies. One thing he did *not* like was the daily work of having to dig worms in order to receive nourishment and stay alive. You can imagine how excited he was when one day, soaring high above the earth, he saw a little man dressed in a scarlet coat walking down the road and hollering "Earth worms for sale. Earth worms traded for skylark feathers." The skylark zoomed down and said to the man, "What's the *deal*?"

"Two worms for one feather," the man answered. "Try it, you'll like it! It's a good deal!" So the skylark tried it and he liked it. He had so many feathers, after all, who's going to miss one feather? He plucked a feather out, got his worms, and had a lot more time to just coast around that day. Day after day, the skylark plucked another feather and traded it for worms. Then the awful day came when he tried to fly but was barely able to get himself off the ground and came crashing down again. He realized what had happened. He was a *bedraggled* skylark, unable to fly, A contradiction in terms—a skylark that can't fly. And so he spent the whole day digging feverishly for worms. When evening came, the little man in the scarlet coat came by. The skylark said to him anxiously, "I've got to trade *back*." The little man just kept on walking, laughing as he went and shouting over his shoulder, "No deal, friend. Worms for feathers is my business, not feathers for worms."

We, like the skylark, are vulnerable to Satan's "deals." When we give ground to Satan, even an inch at a time (or a feather at a time), he wins and we lose. We can find ourselves in hard times, bound down to earth instead of soaring in the heavens, because Satan has had influence in our lives.

It may be that you are suffering from some kind of demonic activity. Satan will go to great lengths to thwart God's goal in our lives and to ruin our testimony. That is why Peter warns us to watch out for the "roaring lion" (1 Peter 5:8). In the next verse he lists three positive steps to take. He writes: 1) "Resist him, steadfast in the faith, knowing that the same sufferings are experienced by your brotherhood in the world" (1 Peter 5:9). We are to resist Satan. That indicates an effort, a struggle, a battle on our part. When he whispers anything contrary to God or godliness, resist him. 2) We are to remain "steadfast in the faith." This indicates not only the idea of trusting and living by faith, but also continually obeying the Word as indicated by "*the* faith." 3) We are to recognize that "the same sufferings are experienced by (our) brotherhood in the world." We are not in this struggle alone. We have God on our side, we have His Spirit within (1 John 4:4!), we have God's armor (Eph. 6:10–20), and we have each other. Satan is no match for a believer thus armed.

You have protection against the wiles and fiery darts of the devil. Don't let your guard down. Keep trusting. If God allows you to suffer through demonic activity, remember that He holds them on a leash, He holds you in His hands and He holds in store a blessing for all who place their trust in Him.

BECAUSE OF UNKNOWN AND UNEXPLAINED REASONS

As mentioned in chapter one, sin in general is always a contributing factor to our woes. It is not always possible, however, to fit our problem into one of the seven other specific categories. There are times even after diligent soul-searching and prayer that the best we can say is "I don't know."

It is not a cop-out to say we don't understand and we don't know everything. It is an admission of our humanness and our finiteness. To bring us to such a conclusion could be reason enough for our adversity. We are not God. We do not and cannot know everything. There will be times, especially in our suffering, when we will be forced to look elsewhere than inside for the answers, and if the answers are not forthcoming or apparent, to trust still.

Trusting in God is more important than knowing. Our trust comes not in that we know all things, but that our God does and that He has our best interest in mind. Faith is "the evidence (or confidence) of things not seen" (Hebrews 11:1). There are many things which we do not know and cannot see but "we walk by faith, not by sight" (2 Corinthians 5:7).

We are naturally much more comfortable walking by sight. It is the only way the old man knows how to walk and he rebels at any change.

There is something within us that demands to know the source of every hurt. The flesh would fight with its puny power rather than yield the field to the new man.

It is not a sin or evil to want to know why we suffer. It can become a problem, though, when we place our desire for this knowledge as a higher priority than our willingness to trust. It might be good for us to ask ourselves in the midst of adversity, "If I could choose between knowing and trusting, which would it be?" The answer to that question may tell us much about where we really are spiritually.

We, unlike God, are not omniscient. But instead of sorrowing in that we are limited in our knowledge, we should be rejoicing that our God has no such limits! Paul, rejoicing in this very fact, wrote in Romans 11:33: "Oh, the depth of the riches both of the wisdom and knowledge of God! How unsearchable are His judgments and His ways past finding out!" The prophet Isaiah had expressed the same idea centuries before by these words:

> For My thoughts are not your thoughts, nor are My ways your ways, says the Lord. For as the heavens are higher than the earth, so are My ways higher than your ways, and My thoughts than your thoughts.
> (Isaiah 55:8–9)

I'm sure we would all agree that it is much more important that God knows than that we know.

Since God's ways are higher than our ways and indeed "past finding out," we cannot and should not expect to understand all that He brings into our lives or allows to happen to us. A toddler has a higher probability of understanding a nuclear physicist explain fission than men do of understanding the ways of God. It is not that we cannot understand *any* of His ways; it is that we cannot understand *all* of His ways.

Our God is gracious to reveal certain things to us. He has revealed all we need to know (2 Peter 1:2–3) but not all we may desire to know. Moses wrote that "the secret things belong unto the Lord our God: but those things which are revealed belong unto us and to our children forever, that we may do all the words of this law" (Deut. 29:29). There are "secret things" which belong only to God. The reason why we are undergoing a particular adversity may be one of them. God is concerned, not that we figure out the secret things, but "that we may do all the words of this law." Do we share the same concern?

Even if God were to explain why we were suffering we might not understand. It might be too far beyond our finite minds. Our level of comprehension cannot hope to match the surpassing wisdom of His eternal decrees. Sinful beings such as we cannot hope to fully discover His holy purpose. The closer we are to Christlikeness, the more we may understand, but we will never fully arrive.

It should not be seen as a bad thing not to know why we are facing adversity. In fact, it should be seen as a good thing. If it was good and right for us to know, do we suppose our heavenly Father would withhold the information? Consider this teaching by Jesus in Matthew 7:9–11:

> Or what man is there among you who, if his son asks for bread, will give him a stone? Or if he asks for a fish, will he give him a serpent? If you then, being evil, know how to give good gifts to your children, how much more will Father who is in heaven give good things to those who ask Him!

It should be noted that these verses follow Jesus' invitation to ask, seek, and know (Matthew 7:7–8). If it is good (in God's opinion!) for us to know, He will certainly reveal it to us. If it is not good for us to know, He will withhold that information. Do we want Him to give us that which is not good?

It *seems* good to us that we should know and understand why we suffer. God, however, sees all the pieces of the puzzle and has long determined how and when and where they will all come together. He knows when and if we will be able to handle the information. He knows our spiritual condition and what is most needful for its development. He knows our receptivity and openness. He knows our level of trust. He knows what our reactions would and would not be. He knows what is harmful and what is helpful. He knows what is in our best interest. He knows how He will use us and our testimony in the future. He knows the impact of our lives, including our suffering, on others. He knows our limits. He knows what information would crush us and what information would build us up. He knows the desires of our heart. He knows our capacity to understand. It may seem good that we should know, but our Father is the best judge of that.

My wife, Sherrie, and I had looked forward with eager anticipation to serving the Lord in the Central African Republic. We, along with our three children, spent almost three years in preparation for this opportunity. I resigned a successful and enjoyable pastorate. We sold our house and most of our furnishings and used the income to help get us to the field. We spent a year in France learning the French language. We finally made it to Africa. We were just getting our feet wet in the ministry when we realized that Sherrie was having an ongoing health problem. It was the kind of problem many ladies would pay good money to have—she continually lost weight no matter how much she ate. Our medical staff set a bottom limit of 92 pounds. When she reached that level we were to go home. We tried all we could do and asked God to intervene. The weight loss continued. It was slow—just one or two pounds a week—but it would not stop.

Those were some real soul-searching days. We understood that our lives and our health and our ministry were all in God's hands. What we could not understand was why this was happening. Our interest was not just "why" medically, but "why" spiritually—in terms of God's will and purpose for us. In the midst of my anguish and crying out to God "why, why?!" He gave me a settled peace by causing me to understand that I did not need to know why; I only needed to trust.

I cannot say that my wife then started to improve. She continued to lose weight and shortly reached the minimum level. We were sent back to the United States where my wife almost immediately started to regain strength and weight. The doctors suggested an inability for her body to adjust to the African climate plus adverse reactions to the anti-malarial medication as the reasons for the weight loss. Not being able to control the climate in Africa (or anywhere!), we realized our days of missionary service there were indeed over.

We had a disappointment that things had not worked out as we had thought and planned and hoped and dreamed. But still we had the settled peace because we knew that God knew why it had all happened. We were and are still completely in His hands. He never makes a mistake and He certainly did not with us. We still do not understand why things happened the way they did. We may never know. To tell you the truth, we aren't even asking anymore. When and if God desires to reveal that part of His perfect and sovereign will to us, I will be a ready listener. Until then I have something even better to do—trust Him.

We fear the unknown. That may be why the unexplained and unknown reasons for our adversity are so upsetting to us. It is easier to be brave in the light than in the dark. Actually, bravery is not called for in the light and can only be known and proved in the dark. Likewise, our faith is not proved by how we handle the days that are full of certainty and light, but how we handle the days that are dark and full of questioning. Gold is purified, not at a comfortable room temperature, but under intense heat.

We as believers have a recourse when fear of the unknown assails us. We can and should run straight to our Father's arms.

During the terrible days of the German Blitz, a father, holding his small son by the hand, ran from a building that had been struck by a bomb. In the front yard was a shell hole. Seeking shelter as quickly as possible, the father jumped into the hole and held up his arms for his son to follow. Terrified, yet hearing his father's voice telling him to jump, the boy replied, "I can't see you!" The father, looking up against the sky tinted red by the burning buildings, called to the silhouette of his son, "But I can see you. Jump!" The boy jumped because he trusted his father. The Christian faith enables us to face life or meet death, not because we can see, but because we can have certainty that we are seen; not that we know all the answers, but that we are known.

Notes

[1]Bauer, Arndt and Gingrich, *A Greek-English Lexicon of the New Testament and Other Early Christian Literature,* 2nd ed. (Chicago: The University of Chicago, 1979), p. 97.

[2]Keil and Delitzsch, *Commentary on the Old Testament,* Vol. 1 (reprint; Grand Rapids, MI: Eerdmans, 1986), pp. 85–86.

[3]Gary Inrig, *A Call to Excellence* (Wheaton, IL: Scripture Press, 1985), p. 56.

[4]Hal Lindsey, *Satan Is Alive And Well On Planet Earth* (Grand Rapids, MI: Zondervan, 1972), pp. 159–62.

[5]Homer Kent, Jr., *Jerusalem To Rome* (Winona Lake, IN: BMH Books, 1972), p. 53.

[6]John MacArthur, *Matthew 16:23* in the MacArthur New Testament Commentary Series (Winona Lake, IN: BMH Books, 1988), p. 41.

PART TWO

How to Respond to Adversity

We may never know or understand all the reasons why we face certain adversities. God in His infinite wisdom and compassion may deem it best to spare us some of the details. Perhaps knowing more would cause us more pain. Perhaps knowing more would cause us to trust less. Perhaps knowing more would alter the response our Lord intends for us to give. Whatever God's purpose, we must face the fact that we may never know "why," at least on this side of heaven.

There is another question besides "why" which should occupy an even larger portion of our concern when we are faced with adversity. That larger question is, "How should I respond?" It is not essential that I know why I am suffering. Understanding the cause or purpose of the adversity may be a definite aid in determining the correct response. If, for example, I determine that I am suffering because of personal sin and the Father's chastisement for that sin, my response (or at least what it *should* be) becomes quite evident. Knowing the reason for the problem, however, is not much use if we do not apply the cure! Our goal thus becomes not "why" but "how should I respond." The "why" may be helpful but it is not essential. It can serve as a pointer or a sign to the right response but it does not replace the right response. Further, not knowing "why" does not negate our obligation to respond correctly to our adversity. Imagine a truck headed straight toward you at a high speed and out of control. How much time would you spend in trying to determine why you were experiencing this difficulty in your life? Which would be more important, knowing why or moving out of the way? Thus it is with all of our adversities; the correct response can be aided by the correct understanding of the situation but it is not limited to it.

It is helpful to note that there is a clear distinction between a temptation and a trial. A temptation is an invitation to evil. A trial is an invitation to obedience. A temptation has character destruction as its purpose. A trial has character construction as its purpose. A temptation leads to less godliness. A trial leads to more Christlikeness. A temptation can result in spiritual pollution. A trial can result in spiritual refinement. A temptation may seem good and yet result in suffering. A trial may seem like suffering and yet result in our good. Our response to temptation is to run away from it to God. We are to flee temptation (1 Tim. 6:11; 2 Tim. 2:22; 1 Cor. 6:18; Job 1:1). Our response to a trial is to remain steadfast in God. The responses suggested in this section all fall under the category of responding to trials. God designs, sends, and uses trials in our lives, but never temptations (James 1:13).

The correct response to adversity does not consist of a narrow choice from the list below. It is not enough to say, for example, "I need to be steadfast and trusting." That is certainly true, but there are other responses equally correct and valuable. Ideally, the correct response will include most if not all of the following:

1. We need to view Christ as the center of our lives.
2. We need to recognize God at work in our lives.
3. We need to look for the good in everything.
4. We need to examine our lives for unconfessed sin.
5. We need to pray.
6. We need to trust.

7. We need to be content in the situation.
8. We need to be patient.
9. We need to be steadfast
10. We need to be joyful.
11. We need to anticipate God's working and claim God's promises.
12. We need to do what we can.

The author is acutely aware that these appropriate responses are much easier to write than to live. The difficulty of the task does not, however, change its necessity. It believe it was G. K. Chesterton who said, "Christianity has not been tried and found wanting; it has been found difficult and not tried." The Bible offers no quick fixes or easy recipes. We are called to commitment. The standard before us is exceedingly high and not easily attained. Indeed, it is a lifelong process, a continual journey and an unending battle. Our goal is not merely to be better; it is to be like Christ (Romans 8:28–30; Ephesians 4:13; 1 Peter 1:13–16). Take comfort and encouragement, however, from 2 Peter 1:3 which reminds us that "His divine power has given to us all things that pertain to life and godliness, through the knowledge of Him who called us by glory and virtue." It may be hard to endure the adversity, much less respond correctly, but we have all that we need not only to survive but to be victorious. We have God's Word, God's Spirit within, God's grace in ever sufficient measure, God's promises, God's people, God's faithfulness, God's love, and God's Son who was "despised and rejected by men, a man of sorrows and acquainted with grief" (Isaiah 53:3).

No matter how difficult the struggle, we know the outcome. We win because Jesus won (John 16:33; Romans 8:35–39; 1 John 5:4–5). The victory includes our eventual Christlikeness (1 John 3:2) and the realization that "the sufferings of this present time are not worthy to be compared with the glory which shall be revealed in us" (Romans 8:18). It will be worth it all, as the old hymn says, when we see Jesus. Even on the temporal and secular level we get a taste of what it means for the victory to exceed the price.

In the 1976 Olympics in Montreal, a Japanese gymnast, Shun Fujimoto, was competing in the team competition. Somehow, during the floor exercises, he broke his right knee. It was obvious to all reasonable observers that he would be forced to withdraw. But they reckoned without the determination of a true competitor. On the following day, Fujimoto competed in his strongest event, the rings. His routine was excellent, but the critical point lay ahead—the dismount. Without hesitation, Fujimoto ended with a twisting, triple somersault. There was a moment of intense quiet as he landed with tremendous impact on his wounded knee. Then came thundering applause as he stood his ground. Later, reporters asked about that moment and he replied, "The pain shot through me like a knife. It brought tears to my eyes. But now I have a gold medal and the pain is gone."[1]

How we respond to suffering and adversity will go a long way in determining what kind of life and testimony we will have. It is not the pressure which counts; it is where it moves us. Are we growing closer to or more distant from God? Heat can burn up and consume; it can also refine. May God direct and enable us all to respond correctly for His glory and our good!

A Christian who was in a very difficult circumstance fell on his knees in despair to cry out to God, "When am I going to get out of all these trials?" But by a slip of the tongue he actually prayed, "What am I going to get out of all these trials?" The change of that one word "when" to "what" was just what the Lord wanted and the hard-pressed Christian needed. There is something more important than escaping our trials—it is learning what our Heavenly Father wants us to gain from them.

WE NEED TO VIEW CHRIST AS THE CENTER OF OUR LIVES TO THE POINT THAT EVERYTHING ELSE, EVEN OUR HEALTH AND LIFE, BECOMES OF SECONDARY IMPORTANCE.

Dan had it made. Dan the man was young, energetic, outgoing, handsome, smart, and athletic. He was moving up in the business world at a fast clip. His marriage appeared to be a model one. He was faithful to church and was looked to as a leader by his peers. But then the bottom fell out. The company he worked for, in making some risky investments, went downhill fast. Dan was without a job. The job market was a poor one and he could not find another position. Dan became bitter. He rejected his friends' advice. He became a stranger to church. He questioned God.

Maria did not have it made. Her life was a soap opera. She had experienced (and could quote in detail) much tribulation. When her

77

husband finally left her for another woman, she could not bring herself to attend church. What would others say and think? Besides, she had chronic health problems which preoccupied her continually. How could she concentrate on God or His Word?

Both Dan and Maria had a common problem. Even though they professed faith in Christ, something else reigned supreme in their hearts. For Dan it was success. His whole life was centered around achievement. His ambition was for others to recognize that he was on top. Maria was the opposite. She gloried in defeat. Her whole life and every conversation was centered around her problems. Her ambition was for others to recognize her suffering and to sympathize with her. Both wanted recognition. *They* were at the center of their lives.

If Jesus Christ is our Lord, He must have first place in every aspect of our lives. As Paul put it: "He is the head of the body, the church, who is the beginning, the firstborn from the dead, that in all things He may have the preeminence." The word "preeminence" means "first place." The word is used only one other time in the New Testament. In Third John, verse 9, we read of Diotrephes "who loves to have the preeminence." First place in our hearts, our devotion and our lives belongs to God alone (Exodus 20:3; Deuteronomy 6:4–5; Luke 14:26; Matthew 10:37). We must be on guard lest we or anyone or anything would take over that sacred spot. We must constantly ask ourselves "Who is first in my life? Who is most important?"

Our natural tendency is to let our problem take over center stage. Our emotions, our decisions, our actions and reactions, our efforts, our time and our concerns all become focused on the problem. Our life is ruled by The Problem. It has been my experience that this set of circumstances inevitably leads to depression. If you are depressed, the first question to ask yourself is "where is my focus?" If it is on the problem, you are only compounding the difficulty of finding the solution. We don't want to go to the other extreme of ignoring the problem. It is good and right and healthy to be open about the problem and to discuss it. The question is not "is it there?" but "what position in my life does it occupy?" Much of modern psychology invites us to look deep within to come to grips with the source of our pain. The Bible invites us to look to God that we might know the Source of our hope. Our problem is

We Need to View Christ as the Center of Our Lives to the Point that Everything Else, Even Our Health and Life, Becomes of Secondary Importance.

not that we have not examined ourselves and our trials enough but that we have allowed their presence to obscure the presence of Christ. When Isaiah was given a glimpse of God in His glory (Isaiah 6), all thoughts of his present needs and trials escaped him except for his unworthiness to stand before God.

As believers, we should gladly view Christ as Lord of all. He does not accept second place and we should not offer Him less than the best. When Christ is the center of our lives, i.e., when all we do revolves around Him, it brings glory to God. But that is not all. This mindset and heart devotion is also definitely for our good as well. It places us in a "no lose" situation. Whatever happens to us, we win. That is what Paul told the Philippians when he wrote "for me to live is Christ, and to die is gain" (Philippians 1:21). What Paul meant by the phrase "to live is Christ" is that Christ meant everything to him. Jesus had the preeminence, first place, in Paul's life. If he were set free from prison and escaped the penalty of death, he would continue to live his Christ-centered life. He would win. If he were put to death, he would be with his Lord (2 Corinthians 5:1–8) and that would be "gain" and indeed "far better" (Philippians 1:23). In other words, he would win. To be able to say "to live is Christ" is to be able to say "to die is gain."

What is really of most importance in your life? Perhaps you can with zest and honesty sing the words of Rhea Miller:

I'd rather have Jesus than silver or gold,
I'd rather be His than have riches untold;
I'd rather have Jesus than houses or lands,
I'd rather be led by His nail-pierced hand
Than to be the king of a vast domain
Or be held in sin's dread sway;
I'd rather have Jesus than anything
This world affords today.

Is Jesus more important to you than anything? Is He more important than your problem? If He is, then make sure that He is the center of your life and the One upon whom you are focusing your attention right now! To focus on the problem means despair. To focus on Christ means hope.

When I was twelve years old, I became lost in the jungles of Panama. The further I went, the thicker the brush and vines and trees became. It became increasingly difficult to tell where I was or where I should be going. I had just about given up hope when I noticed a jet overhead. I waved. They didn't. But the thought struck me that I knew where they were going. There was an airstrip on the base where my father was stationed. More jets passed over. Most of them were going in one direction, and seemed to be getting ready to land. The airstrip, and home, must be that way! How I got into and then out of the jungle is a long story, but I eventually made it home safe, thanks to my guides above. Sometimes we get so bogged down in our problem that it becomes all we see. To find our way home, we need to look above. Our focus needs to shift from our problem to our Lord.

If we have everything except Christ, we are poor indeed. If we have nothing except Christ, we are rich beyond measure. Consider this story of Carl and Hans:[2]

A rich landowner named Carl loved to ride his horse Rajah through his vast estate so that he could congratulate himself on his wealth. One day while on such a ride, he came upon Hans, an old tenant farmer who had sat down to eat his lunch in the shade of a great oak tree.

Hans didn't notice the approaching horseman at first because his head was bowed in prayer. When he did look up, he said, "Oh, excuse me, sir. I didn't see you. I was giving thanks for my food."

"Hmph!" snorted Carl, noticing the coarse dark bread and cheese constituting the old man's lunch. "If that were all I had to eat, I don't think I would feel like giving thanks."

"Oh," replied Hans, "it is quite sufficient. But it is remarkable that you should come by today, sir. I . . . I feel I should tell you, I had a strange dream just before awakening this morning."

"And what did you dream?" Carl asked with an amused smile.

"Well, it wasn't all that clear, sir. You know how dreams are. It seemed there was beauty and peace and music all around, and yet I could hear a voice saying, 'The richest man in the valley will die tonight.' In fact, that was the one part of the dream that was clear, and I woke with those words on my mind."

By now the amused smile had faded from Carl's face and he was frowning.

We Need to View Christ as the Center of Our Lives to the Point that Everything Else, Even Our Health and Life, Becomes of Secondary Importance.

"I don't know what it means, sir," Hans continued. "Perhaps nothing. But I thought I ought to tell you."

"Dreams!" cried the landowner, "Nonsense!" And he turned and galloped away.

"Lord, have mercy on his soul if he really is to die so soon," Hans prayed as he watched horse and rider disappear.

Carl galloped Rajah only a short distance and then slowed the beautiful Arabian to a walk. *Die tonight?* It was ridiculous, of course. No use his going into a panic. That kind of reaction was what made such predictions come true. If he went galloping like a fool through the forest, he probably would fall and break his neck. The best thing to do about the old man's dream was to forget it.

But he couldn't forget it. Die tonight? How could he, sitting perfectly safe now in his own home? He felt fine. At least he had felt fine until Hans described his stupid dream. Now he didn't feel too well.

For a while he debated with himself about it, but finally that evening he called his doctor, who was also a personal friend. "Could you come over?" he asked. "I need to talk with you."

When the doctor arrived, Carl told him the whole story. "Sounds like poppycock to me," the doctor said, "but for your peace of mind, let's examine you."

A little later, his examination complete, the doctor was full of assurances. "Carl, you're as strong and healthy as that horse of yours. There's no way you're going to die tonight." He chuckled, "Unless you shoot yourself or something like that."

Carl didn't think his friend's remark was terribly funny.

"Look," said the doctor, "if it will make you feel any better, I'll be glad to stay awhile."

The two friends visited for an hour or so and then played cards through the night. As dawn broke, Carl thanked his friend and told him how foolish he felt for being upset by an old man's dream.

It was about 9 a.m. when a messenger arrived at Carl's door. "It's old Hans," the messenger said. "He died last night in his sleep."

The richest man in the valley had not been the one with vast holdings, but the man of simple faith in Jesus Christ.

Our first response to adversity is to view Christ as the center of our lives to the point that everything else, even our health and life, becomes of secondary importance. Yielding everything up to God, casting all our care upon Him (1 Peter 5:7), focusing our attention upon our Lord and looking unto Jesus as the author and finisher of our faith (Hebrews 12:2) are all involved in viewing Christ as the center of our lives. It is necessary because without it we become mired and weighted down. It is necessary because it opens the door for all the other responses referred to in this section. Without this step, without this response, your problems become compounded. With this step comes light to replace darkness and hope to replace despair. Look up!

Remember Dan and Maria? Dan came to realize that little by little success and money had come to usurp the throne of his heart where Christ should have reigned. His response was eventually to commit his life to the lordship of Christ. He did not get his old job back. He had to move into a different house. He went into a completely different kind of business where he made less money to begin with but also experienced less stress and more security. He is not looked up to now merely for who he is and what he has; he is highly regarded because of what Christ means in his life. His life is a testimony of the power of Christ.

Through the influence of some concerned Christian friends, Maria came to realize that she had told everyone except God about her difficulties. These friends helped her all they could and all the while pointed her toward God. Maria's response was to start living for God instead of for Maria. What a change! As she ministered to others her problems seemed to take less of a toll on her and her health improved. Several people in her family came to know Jesus as Lord and Savior. Her problems did not go away, but as she honored Christ, He blessed her life with grace and strength and enablement for each day.

When we focus on our problems, we have despair. When we focus on our Lord, we have hope. For His glory and our good, we must view Christ as the center of our lives.

WE NEED TO RECOGNIZE GOD AT WORK IN OUR LIVES

"I had been my whole life a bell,
And never knew it until at that moment
I was lifted and struck"

—Annie Dillard

If another believer tells you that God is blessing him, you've got to know how to interpret that message. Usually it's just a matter of figuring out the main area of concern in the life of the "blessee."

At a minister's conference, if a pastor says that God is blessing, generally the translation is, "our attendance and giving are up."

At a businessmen's breakfast, if an executive says that God is blessing, predictably the translation is, "our sales are up"

At a hospital, if a patient says that God is blessing, usually the translation is, "I'm feeling better."

In a home, if the mother says that God is blessing, most likely the translation is, "there are no major disciplinary problems at the moment."

If things are going well, then we conclude that God must be blessing. If things are not going so well, then we are silent on the issue. God's blessings are somehow elevated to the positive occurrences alone. It is as if God had control over only one part of our lives. When negative things

83

come our way we tend to wonder where they came from and how they got there. Surely, they could not be heaven-sent!

It may well be that the church's attendance and giving are up because of God's blessing. But what about a church that is apostate, or a cult that experiences the same apparent growth—is God also blessing them? Is growth the indicator of God's blessing?

It may well be that a Christian businessman is enjoying increased sales due to God's blessing. But what about ungodly businesses and the pornography industries which are booming—is more money an accurate barometer of God's blessing?

It may well be that a patient is improving, thanks to God's gracious intervention and blessing in his life. But what about the unbeliever in the next bed who is also improving—is God also restoring his health? Is good health an adequate sign of God's blessing?

It may well be that a mother is experiencing God's blessing on her home in that Junior is being obedient. But what about an ungodly mother who, through harshness and the imposition of fear, has an obedient child (at least on the outside)? Is God blessing her tyranny? Is obedience evidence in itself that God is blessing?

God does indeed bless in many positive ways. Certainly, He showers us with more positive blessings than we recognize or take time to thank Him for. A believer should praise God openly for His many and obvious blessings. In fact, this is one way in which believers can be a real testimony for God. If, for example, after you have recovered from surgery, someone should ask if you had a good doctor, you might reply, "Yes, but more importantly, I have a great God!"

James wrote that "every good gift and every perfect gift is from above, and comes down from the Father of lights, with whom there is no variation or shadow of turning" (James 1:17). God is due credit and praise for every good and perfect gift we receive. We usually don't have a problem with that. Our problem is one of definition. We have read into the words "good" and "perfect" the sole idea of positive material blessings. In other words, we judge what is "good" and we decide what the criteria is for a "perfect" gift. On our prejudiced scale, that which is good means that which is in some way better than what we already have (i.e., higher attendance, better health, etc.). But is that what God meant?

The context of James 1:17 is interesting. James had not been discussing what we would normally term as positive blessings! In fact, he was just speaking of trials and temptations. He follows up by pointing out the need to live the Word. He says nothing about getting more camels for your shekels. The good and perfect gifts are not directly connected with those things which we would normally consider positive.

The point is this; we already recognize God at work in our lives in the good times; now we need to see His hand in the "bad" times. If God is chastening because of sin, praise the Lord for His faithfulness and concern and that He treats you as His child! It may not seem pleasant, but it is a blessing. How many children are not "blessed" with parents that care enough about them to chasten them? The writer of Hebrews, at the end of his discussion of the Father's chastening, writes: "Therefore strengthen the hands which hang down, and the feeble knees" (Hebrews 12:12). It should be an encouragement to know that God has dealt with us as sons.

If God is allowing you to go through some trial for the purpose of your character development, praise Him, not because you enjoy the trial or suffering, but because you were counted worthy to be refined. It is not a hunk of rock that is refined, but a piece of gold. It is a blessing to be precious in the Lord's eyes!

When Job's wife suggested that he "curse God and die," he responded, "you speak as one of the foolish women speaks. Shall we indeed accept good from God, and shall we not accept adversity?" To indicate that Job had hit the nail on the head, the verse goes on to say: "In all this Job did not sin with his lips" (Job 1:10). God has the right to send adversity as well as positive blessings. He sends rain as well as sunshine, both of which are vital to growth and life. God knows how much adversity to send and to whom and how long and how severe. He knows the outcome and "as for God, His way is perfect" (Psalm 18:30). Job was not saying he enjoyed the adversity, but that God was in control of all things, even adversity. We need to recognize God at work in the bad as well as the good times.

In Italy, for thirty years under the Borgias, they had warfare, terror, murder and bloodshed. But they produced Michelangelo, Leonardo da Vinci, and the Renaissance. In Switzerland they had brotherly love, they had five hundred years of democracy and peace. What did they produce? The cuckoo clock. Trials often lead to triumph whereas the status quo leads to mediocrity.

It is enlightening to consider the things for which we and others thank God. Seldom have I heard thanks given for trials and adversities. Often they are not brought into public display and when they are, it is usually to pray that they may pass as soon as possible. Adversity is not to be admitted and to be avoided at all cost—at least that is the impression we give. To admit to a problem is to admit to frailty, and we are too proud for that. To admit to adversity might sound as if we are being chastened, and we don't want anyone to think that of us. To speak of a trial we are going through does not bring joy to others and we don't want to be a downer.

The Bible, however, indicates that we should not only speak of these things but actually give thanks for them. Paul expressed this to the Ephesians by writing: ". . . giving thanks always for all things to God the Father in the name of our Lord Jesus Christ" (Ephesians 5:20). It is hard to get around the words "always" and "all things." Could this really be God's will? Paul also wrote: "Rejoice always, pray without ceasing, in everything give thanks; for this is the will of God in Christ Jesus for you" (1 Thess. 5:16–18).

Our lives as God's children are solidly, completely, and eternally in God's hands (John 10:27–30). Our heavenly Father does not disappear when adversity comes. He is not at work in our lives only when we see positive blessings. He never leaves us. He never forsakes us. He never fails us.

While teaching a government course to high school seniors, I asked them a question on a test which I knew they could not answer. We were studying about needing all the facts before making decisions. The question I gave them was missing some facts pertinent to the answer. I wanted to see if they would ask me for the missing information. During the course of the test about half the class raised their hand, one at a time, to ask for help. They realized that they could not do it themselves, that they did not know all the facts and that they needed someone who had both the facts and the ability to help. Just because we face a difficult situation does not mean that God is not there. He is working and He is waiting for us to ask and to trust.

A pastor friend of mine went through a rough time recently in his church. Some ugly and unfortunate things happened. The attendance and offering fell off sharply as a result. An associate pastor, who was a dear friend, was released because of lack of funds to pay his salary. The situation, I thought, was desperate. I had an opportunity to meet with this pastor and to give my sympathy and prayer support. It soon became apparent, however, that even through all that had happened, this pastor was able to see God at work. As it turned out, it was a time of cleansing and reordering of priorities. Those who were left were strengthened and united in the purpose of following after God. The church has since more than regained its losses. God worked despite the negative situation and turned what could have been evil into something beneficial. It was not enjoyable for this pastor or his congregation to go through the adversity and God does not delight in seeing His churches split, but God can use even such difficult situations to bring about His will.

Joseph went through an abundance of bad times and yet glorified God for His hand at work. He declared to his brothers: ". . . you meant evil against me; but God meant it for good, in order to bring it about as it is this day, to save many people alive" (Genesis 50:20).

May the Lord give us open eyes to see that He is at work in our lives in the bad as well as the good times.

WE NEED TO LOOK FOR THE GOOD IN EVERYTHING

To say that it gets hot in the Central African Republic is like saying it gets cool at the North Pole. There was one particular day, however, when the thermometer ran out of numbers and just said "boil." It was on this particular day that I was allowed to accompany some of our mission leaders to the site of the new and first Pygmy church.

We had not realized that this young congregation had already constructed their own church building. They had done so completely on their own and with no funds from the mission. They were beaming with pride as they showed us around. A half acre spot had been cleared from the rain forest. The walls were freshly baked mud blocks. The building was air conditioned. Since the walls were only three feet high and the roof started at five feet, there was a two-foot opening all the way around the building which allowed ample air to flow through and thus supply free air conditioning. The roof was a thatched one, but it was made with freshly cut grass which meant there were few bugs as yet to drop on one's head. The "pews" were logs which had all the bark removed for one's seating enjoyment. The members were called to assemble by the ringing of the church "bell"—an old tire rim hung outside the church on a post and vigorously beaten to the delight of the children and dismay of the goats.

I watched with great joy as their pastor (a tremendous young African named Francois) spoke to them from God's Word. They drank in every word. Joy beamed from their eyes as he explained the privilege of demonstrating love by giving, just as God had done through Jesus (John 3:16; Romans 5:8). The pastor then applied the idea of giving to "these American brothers who have come so far." He suggested that they, these destitute Pygmies, give us an offering! They almost fell over one another trying to get the live chicken (worth two weeks wages to them) to present to our mission director. Our director, Tom Julien, received that gift with as much dignity and gratitude as any statesman might have received a most precious gift. It was a moment to be treasured.

Whenever I now, as a pastor of a church in the U.S.A., have the urge to bemoan the fact that our roof needs to be reshingled, I am grateful to be thinking in terms of shingles instead of grass; or when the pews need to be recovered, I am grateful to be thinking in terms of adding cushions rather than removing bark.

Often we are so focused upon our problems that we fail to see the blessings that we have. We need to look for the good in everything. We should be at least as grateful for the roof we have as we are disgruntled that it needs to be repaired.

This past Christmas season I spent fifty hours one day at a shopping mall. I learned firsthand what it means to be "malled!" When my family and I finally reached the sanctity of our home, I collapsed into a chair, removed my shoes and tried to make peace with my feet and legs, promising not to mistreat them so in the future. In the midst of my moaning and complaining, my eyes happened to meet the amused smile of my sister-in-law. Kathy was not complaining, although she had more reason to than I did. Kathy didn't need to say anything to me; I stopped moaning on my own. You see, Kathy has been confined to a wheelchair (when, at least, she has been healthy enough to be able to get into one) since October 30, 1976. She has been a quadriplegic since she was eighteen years old. For her to have aching legs and feet from too much walking would be a cherished gift too wonderful to imagine. But Kathy didn't complain; she just smiled at me and I quit complaining. I also thanked God that He had given me the grace to walk and Kathy the grace to handle not being able to walk.

We need to look for the good in everything; but be warned, sometimes it is difficult to find! I confess from experience that it is tough in the middle of a crisis to see the silver lining. The sky can become so dark and our vision so clouded that even if we can see a ray of light it seems woefully inadequate. But that is the very reason why we need to "look for" and search out the good in everything. Remember that a shadow is only possible if a light is shining somewhere!

If we were without God in this world, then we would have a reason to be without hope (1 Thess. 4:13; Eph. 2:12). Such, however, is not the case for a believer. Indeed, we not only have God; more importantly, He has us! Based on that, we *can* look for the good in everything.

When spring came to England after the devastating bombing raids of 1941 by Nazi Germany, a strange thing occurred. It brought a beautiful, botanical resurrection. The explosions of the bombs brought to the surface seeds of plants which were thought to be extinct. Some ninety-five different flowers and shrubs were found suddenly growing and blooming in the bomb-pocked landscape of England. Likewise, adversity in life often brings to the surface unexpected and undeveloped parts of our lives. The bombs of adversity and suffering may well resurrect in us long-dormant flowers.

The most often quoted and occasionally misused verse on this subject is Romans 8:28. There Paul writes: "And we know that all things work together for good to those who love God, to those are the called according to His purpose." If we are understanding this verse right, then surely we should look for the good in everything. We need to make sure then that we are understanding what Paul intended to say. We need to keep in mind that this was not just some blind optimism, not just the longing of Paul's heart. This verse, as is true of all Scripture, was given by inspiration of God (2 Timothy 3:16).

When Paul writes, "We know that . . .," he implies that this should be part of our common knowledge, experience, and profession as believers. The truth of this verse should not be foreign to us. If we do not know and believe the message of this verse, it may be time for a spiritual checkup!

The next two words are the toughest. We could easily accept, without much stretching of our faith, that "many things" or perhaps even "most things" work together for good, but God calls us to walk by faith and believe that "all things" are under His domain. A believer who finds a good job has no difficulty with this verse until he is laid off. A new bride accepts this verse until her husband has an affair. Both scream out to know *how* this could possibly be for their *good*.

Part of the answer is, as we have mentioned before, that we see only a piece of the puzzle while God sees it all. We only know, for instance, that we have been laid off and we don't know where the next paycheck will come from. But just because we don't know doesn't mean that God is uninformed. He is not fretting, He knows our needs, He knows the end from the beginning and He is sovereign over all. Do you really believe this in your heart? If not, you know why you have a hard time with this verse.

C.E.B. Cranfield, in his commentary on Romans, has done a superb job of evaluating Paul's thought. In explaining how all things work together for good, he writes:

> But the AV and RV rendering "work together" make too much of the separate meanings of the components of the Greek compound verb: it is better translated by some such expression as "prove advantageous," "be profitable." Paul's meaning is that all things, even those which seem most adverse and hurtful, such as persecution and death itself, are profitable to those who truly love God. But not every sort of profit is meant. So the expression has to be made more precise. Hence the addition of "for their true good." Paul does not mean that all things serve the comfort or convenience or worldly interests of believers: It is obvious that they do not.[3]

Cranfield goes on to explain that these things must serve believers by "confirming their faith and drawing them closer to the Master."[4]

The point is, what we consider good may not be what God considers best or of most profit to us. We have narrow boundaries which often reflect shallow faith and low tolerance. God has a higher ideal and calling for us than we would have set on our own.

Do not misunderstand—God does not consider a husband's unfaithfulness "good." He does not delight in the fact that one of His children has lost his job. We must trust, however, that He is able to work *all things* together to the point that we profit from them. We must learn to count profit by God's register.

Paul qualifies his statements as "to those who love God, to those who are the called according to His purpose." It is hard to visualize *anything* working together for good to those who do not love God. But as we make loving God central in our lives, we can begin to see His mighty hand at work in even the most difficult situations.

Paul ends the verse with the reminder that all of this is "according to His purpose." But what is His purpose? Many have too narrowly understood this to indicate only that it was God's purpose to save us. God has more in mind than just snatching us from the fire. His purpose, as very clearly expressed in the next verse (Romans 8:29), is that we as believers would be conformed to the image of His Son. God is working all things together for *that* purpose. That is what is most profitable for us.

It is apparent that our definition of "good" may have much to do with whether we actually realize the good for which God is working all things together. If, for example, we define "good" in our situation as "deliverance" while God is defining it as "grace," we may totally miss the lesson and the blessing by looking under the wrong rock. In the adversity we face, grace is a more likely tool to conform us to the image of Christ than is deliverance. It is not that God will not deliver us from our adversity, but rather that before deliverance comes, both how it comes and when it comes may contain manifold opportunities to draw us closer to God and work in us the image of His Son.

When a refiner wants to purify a substance, he takes into consideration the fact that the more precious a metal is the harder it is to purify. Therefore, when he attempts to purify a very precious metal he watches it very closely. He never leaves. He makes sure that the fire is hot enough to do its intended purpose and that it does not get too hot. As the process develops, the impurities come to the top of the substance. He skims off the impurities until there are no more left. The refiner knows he has finished when he can look at the purified substance and clearly see his own reflection. The Lord is working all things together for good, by His definition, so that when He looks at your life He will more and more clearly see His own reflection. Consider this reminder of God's refining process: "In this you greatly rejoice, though now for a little while, if need be, you have been grieved by various trials, that the genuineness of your faith, being much more precious than gold that perishes, though it is tested by fire, may be found to praise, honor, and glory at the resurrection of Jesus Christ" (1 Peter 1:6–7).

This process comes about not only as the Refiner looks at us, but also as we look to Him. Paul, in his second letter to the Corinthians, put it this way: "But we all, with unveiled face, beholding as in a mirror the glory of the Lord, are being transformed into the same image from glory to glory, just as by the Spirit of the Lord" (2 Corinthians 3:18).

There is also a very practical side to this topic. Not that our spiritual growth and development are not practical, for they surely are, but that they are harder to discern at times, plus they generally take a while to become evident. There can be, however, more tangible, immediate, and not necessarily spiritual evidence.

This chapter begins with the account of my visit to the Pygmy church. How the day ended carries another illustration. Having finally arrived back at "civilization," I, along with several other missionaries, was invited over for dinner. I was not feeling well but I went anyway. By the time I arrived at our host's home I could do nothing but lie down. I apologized to the host as I was barely able to move much less eat. As I was praying that the Lord would choose this time to rapture His Church and thus deliver me, the host entered with the evening's meal—a platter piled high with fried grasshoppers. "All things work together for good."

The best way to look for the good in everything is to look for God in everything. He is there and He is good.

WE NEED TO EXAMINE OUR LIVES FOR UNCONFESSED SINS SINCE ADVERSITY MAY RELATE TO DISCIPLINE

The story is told of Governor Neff, of Texas, who visited the penitentiary of that state and spoke to the assembled convicts. When he had finished he said that he would remain for a while, and that if any man wanted to speak with him, he would gladly listen. He further announced that he would listen in confidence and that nothing a man might say would be used against him. When the meeting was over a large group of men remained, many of them life-termers. One by one they passed by, each telling the Governor that there had been a frame-up, an injustice or judicial blunder, and each asking that he be freed. Finally, one man came up and said, "Mr. Governor, I just want to say that I am guilty. I did what they sent me here for. But I believe I have paid for it, and if I were granted the right to get out, I would do everything I could to be a good citizen and show myself worthy of your mercy." He was freed.

Our Lord desires for us to own up to our sins. He wants us not only to admit to them, but to repent of them. To bring that about, He will often allow us to suffer the consequences of our sin, whether directly or indirectly, plus He will allow our fellowship (though not our relationship) with Him to be broken.

Since this is true, it is certainly to our advantage to seek to remedy the situation as soon as possible. Our spiritual vitality and growth are dependent upon swift action. Also, on a human level, we don't want to suffer needlessly.

We must keep in mind that a quick apology, which issues from the mouth and not from the heart, does not fool God. Even as a gullible parent, I can usually determine the level of sincerity in my children. If our motivation is just to get out from under the negative consequences of our sin, rather than to be truly repentant, we have gained no ground, no matter how loudly we vocalize our apology.

The Apostle John gives valuable insight into this issue in his first Epistle. A brief examination of 1 John 1:4–10 is necessary in order to formulate a proper biblical foundation for confession. Other passages, as we shall see, address the topic, but this passage appears to be the most informative. John writes as follows:

And these things we write to you that your joy may be full.

This is the message which we have heard from Him and declare to you, that God is light and in Him is no darkness at all.

If we say that we have fellowship with Him, and walk in darkness, we lie and do not practice the truth.

But if we walk in the light as He is in the light, we have fellowship with one another, and the blood of Jesus Christ His Son cleanses us from all sin.

If we say that we have no sin, we deceive ourselves, and the truth is not in us.

If we confess our sins, He is faithful and just to forgive us our sins and to cleanse us from all unrighteousness.

If we say that we have not sinned, we make Him a liar, and His word is not in us.

(1 John 1:4–10)

We Need to Examine our Lives for Unconfessed Sins
Since Adversity May Relate to Discipline

This passage, though talking about a dark subject (namely, our sins and their effect), glows with good news. There is the message of hope and cure and forgiveness alongside the warning.

Verse four expresses the purpose of what follows. We are given a glimpse into the Father's heart as we read the words He has given through the Apostle John: "these things we write to you that your joy may be full." Our heavenly Father delights to see His children full of joy. He knows, however, that true joy will only come to those who are in a right relationship and fellowship with Him. The right relationship is established by new birth. When we confess Jesus Christ as Lord and Savior, we become children of God (John 1:12–13; Romans 10:9–13). This is a relationship which is unending (John 5:24, 10:27–30; Romans 8:1; Ephesians 1:3–14). The right relationship has to do with coming to the Light. The right fellowship, however, has to do with walking in the light. Coming to the Light (Jesus) is a once-for-all action. It is a decision that is made, and the moment after it is made it becomes a past action which has established one's eternal destiny. It is similar to a train going down the tracks—a switch is thrown and the train changes tracks and direction. It is not a gradual thing which may or may not happen. Someone threw the switch. The train changed tracks based upon that past decision and action. One rail of the track is God's predestination, having chosen us in Him before the foundation of the world. The other rail of the track is man's decision for God, having come under conviction by the Holy Spirit that he is a hell-bound sinner in desperate need of forgiveness from Holy God. The point is, it is a once-for-all transaction and the relationship is eternally established. The train, and our lives, will end up at a different destination based upon that decision.

As we have seen, John offers the possibility "that your joy may be full." I believe that John assumes that his readers have a right relationship with God, since he repeatedly refers to them as children of God (see 3:1–2, as an example). The emphasis in this passage, then, is that they maintain the right fellowship with God and thus continue to be full of joy.

Walking in the light, in contrast to coming to the Light, is a continual discipline. Walking in the light means living daily according to God's standards. It is not an option for a believer, but is rather expected

(John 8:12, 12:46; Ephesians 5:8–17). There are, in fact, consequences to pay for not walking in the light. The believer will suffer, among other things, a break in fellowship with God, and that is John's point in this passage.

A proper understanding of our need for confession does not begin with an introspective look at our own life. It always begins with a correct and awe-inspiring view of a holy God. That is exactly what happened when Isaiah was allowed to see God on His throne (Isaiah 6). Isaiah, upon realizing the awesome holiness of God, could only see himself as a sinner. The only words that came out of his mouth were, "Woe is me, for I am undone! Because I am a man of unclean lips, and I dwell in the midst of a people of unclean lips; for my eyes have seen the King, the Lord of hosts" (Isaiah 6:5).

We need to recapture that heavenly and true vision of God. We will not likely truly repent until we do. That is why John, before calling for confession, writes that "God is light and in Him is no darkness at all" (1 John 1:5). He is utterly and completely holy. He is not just a good buddy who winks at our sin. Sin is an affront to a holy God. It is only His great grace and mercy that keeps us from being cast headlong into the eternal flames of hell. One cannot long contemplate the holiness of God without falling before Him in adoration and confession.

Because God is holy, and because we are His children, He expects us to be holy. Peter writes that we must be "as obedient children, not conforming yourselves to the former lusts, as in your ignorance; but as He who called you is holy, you also be holy in all your conduct" (1 Peter 1:14–15). A little further on, Peter adds that God has called us "out of darkness into His marvelous light" (1 Peter 2:9). That is also John's thought as he goes on to say: "If we say that we have fellowship with Him, and walk in darkness, we lie and do not practice the truth" (1 John 1:6). There is no way that we can have fellowship with God if we are walking in darkness. God desires us to have fellowship with Him and so He constantly guides us in the light and pulls us back when we tend to wander into the darkness.

In verse seven, John indicates that walking in the light results not only in fellowship with God, but also with God's children. Joy comes from being in harmony with our Father and with our brothers and sisters in Christ.

We Need to Examine our Lives for Unconfessed Sins
Since Adversity May Relate to Discipline

Rejecting the notion that we are sinners (v. 8) or that we have been guilty of sin (v. 10) does not result in joy. John very directly points out that if that is our case, "we deceive ourselves, and the truth is not in us" (v. 8), and "we make Him a liar, and His word is not in us" (v. 10.)

Walking in darkness results in broken fellowship with God and each other. Refusing to face up to our sin only makes matters worse. There is only one option for the one who has strayed into the darkness—confession.

One of the great promises of the Bible, and a most tremendous blessing for us as believers, is contained in 1 John 1:9: "If we confess our sins, He is faithful and just to forgive us our sins and to cleanse us from all unrighteousness." God has supplied the cure. We do not need to continue in the dark. There is forgiveness and there is light. Confession is the key.

In order to cause us to realize the need to confess and to restore that precious fellowship with God, He will allow us to suffer. He may very well send a particular adversity to get our attention and thus to get us back into fellowship with Him.

It may be that you have already confessed all the known sins in your life. That, of course, does not mean that there are not any others, but simply that you are not aware of them. Does that let you off the hook? Does God then say, "That's okay, since you were not really aware?" No sin is acceptable to God. If you are not aware of a particular sin, God may be using your circumstances to bring it into clearer view.

King David was aware of the need to come to grips with sins which might otherwise go for a while undetected. Left to themselves they do not dissolve, but rather fester and eventually produce more problems. In Psalm 19 David wrote: "Who can understand his errors? Cleanse me from secret faults" (v. 12). David concludes Psalm 139 with this petition: "Search me, O God, and know my heart; try me and know my anxieties; and see if there be any wicked way in me, and lead me in the way everlasting" (vv. 23–24). God, Who knows our thoughts even before we think them (Ps. 139:2), knows our every sin and is certainly capable of revealing them to us.

God wants us to go beyond mere confession of sin in our life. He wants us to go beyond recognition of specific sins. He wants us to press on to repentance. Repentance is more than acknowledging sin; it is abandoning sin. A Sunday school teacher once asked her class what was meant by the word "repentance." A little boy put up his hand and said, "It is being sorry for your sins." A little girl also raised her hand and said, "It is more than that, it is being sorry enough to quit."

Consider the case where a believer has repented of all known sins, he has searched his heart and has asked God to reveal any unknown sins to him, he has acknowledged and repented of those, and yet there is no change in his trial, no release from adversity. What are we then to conclude? How should he then proceed? I would like to suggest two possibilities.

In the first place, the adversity may not be related to the sin. As we have seen (John 9, etc.), not all adversity is related to sin. That does not mean that the person undergoing some trial has not sinned, but that a specific sin is not the cause of the problem. There is, of course, the continuing and lingering effect of sin in general in our world, and as we have stated elsewhere, that is always a factor. However, we are thinking here more in terms of specific individual sin. It is only by God's grace that we do not suffer the consequences of each of our sins. As David wrote, "He has not dealt with us according to our sins, nor punished us according to our iniquities" (Ps. 103:10). Therefore, it is quite possible to face an adversity which has no direct link to a specific sin problem in our life. In that case, though it is *always* right, proper and necessary to repent, there might not be a change in a person's situation just because they do so.

Secondly, God may have a further purpose in allowing the adversity to linger. In that case, the adversity may not be related to sin at all (as described above) or it may be related to a specific sin God wants us to face *and* another area in our spiritual life. For example, if God was dealing with a certain sin area in my life and He also wanted me to learn to trust Him more, repentance of that sin would only accomplish part of His purpose. That is not to negate or diminish the importance of repentance, but simply to say that God has another step He wants me to take.

My son, Jason, recently taught our poodle puppy to roll over. In the training process he soon learned that he had to take a two-step approach.

We Need to Examine our Lives for Unconfessed Sins
Since Adversity May Relate to Discipline

First, he taught her to lie down, then from that position, to roll over. He could not get her to roll over while she was standing on her feet. Perhaps God wants to get us to our knees in repentance. It is easier to learn His lessons on our knees than on our feet.

WE NEED TO PRAY

A certain general gave up in despair. His army was being attacked by the ruthless enemy who was armed to the teeth with clubs and rocks. The general and his army were armed only with machine guns and atomic weapons. He wasn't sure it was worth the effort to even try. What if it didn't work?

The above scene is a ridiculous one which happens all the time. Countless are the occasions when someone has said to me in despair: "I guess all we can do is pray." Hope is fading fast or gone altogether because all we have left in our arsenal is measly prayer. What good will our atom bomb do against the enemy's sticks?

The problem, of course, is that of not recognizing the power available to us. Because it is not our own power, we sense a lack of control over it. Because it cannot be held, measured and analyzed, we may be skeptical of its existence, much less its ability to actually do anything.

There is power in prayer. The power is not in us nor the eloquence of our wording. The power rests with our Father who always and unfailingly hears us. When a small girl runs to her father yelling, "Daddy, help!," it is not the pleading voice or the words which deliver her, but the father who hears and responds to his daughter's needs. The yell for help is a means for soliciting the father's help. She yells to him because

103

she *knows* he is able to handle problems which are beyond her ability to cope with. So it is when we pray to our Father. The power rests in Him. To respond in despair that "all we can do is pray" may reveal much about our level of trust in our Father's ability to hear and/or respond.

Prayer is not our last resort, but our first and best option. No matter what else we do or don't do, prayer must head our list. If we have time to do only one thing, it must be to pray. If we have time enough to do more than one thing, the first of these must be prayer.

True prayer senses the urgency of the situation. S. D. Gordon wrote: "The greatest agency put into man's hands is prayer. And to define prayer one must use the language of war. Peace language is not equal to the situation."[5] We are involved in spiritual warfare. Our enemy, Satan, desires to cut off our lines of communication. He does so by planting seeds of doubt about the reality or effectiveness of prayer. But those who realize the battle that is being waged cling all the more earnestly to prayer. To be cut off from God means disaster. Satan has no power or authority to cut those lines of communication; he simply gets us to do it.

Our Father, on the other hand, has instructed us to keep the lines open. When adversity comes, he invites us to talk with him about it. It is not that God is unaware and is waiting for the 5 o'clock news for information! He knows all things, but He has chosen to extend to us the privilege of prayer and the blessing of seeing answers to specific prayers. Therefore, He invites us to pray. This idea was best communicated by Paul when he wrote "Be anxious for nothing, but in everything by prayer and supplication, with thanksgiving, let your requests be made known to God" (Philippians 4:6). Notice the absolutes: nothing and everything. Every conceivable situation, problem, adversity, or trial is covered by those two words. We don't just bring little problems or big problems, but all problems to God.

Paul used several words which deserve closer inspection. The first word, translated "prayer," carries with it the idea of worship or adoration. We do not come to God with a list of demands; we come with a heart of praise. The first element in removing our anxiety is reflection on the greatness of God. I have personally found it helpful, when facing an anxious situation, to pause and contemplate just how great God is. It is difficult to truly consider God's "omnies" (He is omnipresent, omnipotent, omniscient, etc.) and hold on to anxiety at the same time. So Paul instructs us to begin with a worshipful type of prayer.

He adds the word "supplication" next. The original meaning of that word (*deesis* in the Greek NT) meant "lack."[6] It presupposes that the person praying recognizes his lack or inability. We come to God in humility, confessing both our unworthiness and our need. We come with prayer and supplication, or, in other words, with adoration and humble entreaty.

Paul goes yet a step further and adds the words "with thanksgiving." It takes a measure of faith to give God thanks at the moment of praying instead of waiting to see how, or if, or when, He will act. Actually, if we do the first two parts (worship and humbly ask) but do not truly believe that God will respond, there will be no lessening of our anxiety. Someone recently told me, "I've prayed and prayed, but God doesn't seem to hear or care." In the first place, to question God's ability to hear or His concern to care is not praying in an attitude of worship! But putting that issue aside for the moment, I asked this person if he believed God would respond. The answer was "I don't know. Maybe He will, and maybe He won't. So far, He hasn't done anything." It was obvious that this individual had not prayed "with thanksgiving." It is important to remember Jesus' words about faith and prayer: "And all things, whatever you ask in prayer, believing, you will receive" (Matthew 21:22). We need to come to the Lord in adoration, in humility, and in faith.

Paul goes on to say "let your requests be made known to God." God invites us, He wants us, to communicate our requests to Him. I believe that includes not only our needs, but also our desires. We need to subject everything to the Father's will and to ask with the right motive. If we want something sinful or potentially harmful to our spiritual life and development, that is not a valid request. Outside of such limitations, however, we should not view God as a miser who gives out only what is essentially needed. In fact, in another passage, Paul says that God ". . . is able to do exceedingly abundantly above all that we ask or think . . ." (Ephesians 3:20). It is good to keep all of this in balance and to "set your mind on things above, not on things on the earth" (Colossians 3:2), and to "seek first the kingdom of God and His righteousness" (Matthew 6:33).

Instead of worrying about a problem, if we would give our requests over to God in adoration, and in humility and in faith, we would then know "the peace of God, which surpasses all understanding" (Philippians 4:7).

Another consideration in our praying is our focus or perspective. Jack Taylor in his book *Prayer: Life's Limitless Reach*, gives the following insight:

> While prayer in one sense is a cycle, it is in another sense a triangle. That triangle has God at one point, the object or problem at another point, and the one praying at the final point. We pray from one of those vantage points. If we pray from the ground of the problem as we see it, we will be problem conscious. If we pray from the ground of ourselves, we will be self-conscious. If we pray from the ground of who God is and what he has done, we will be God-conscious. Problem-consciousness will yield mourning and despair. Self-consciousness will produce guilt and morbid introspection. God-consciousness will bring gladness and purpose as well as victory. Praying from God's vantage point is what I call praying from the ground of redemption.[7]

We have hope and reason to pray because of who God is and what He has done. A problem may overshadow our lives, but God overshadows the problem. We need to see it from His perspective.

That we are to pray and how we are to pray have already been touched on. Next, we need to decide what to pray for. Since every situation is unique, there is no way to specifically answer this question. We can, however, examine some general categories which can then be related to the reader's individual needs. The following areas are not listed in order of priority. The order might change depending on the situation and might include all or only part of the following.

The first item to pray for, as we have already briefly discussed, is our requests (Philippians 4:6). We are to pray at all times (1 Thessalonians 5:17), not just when we have a need or request. We are also to spend time praising God, not just asking for things. But it is proper and even instructed that we should make our requests known to God. In so doing, it is best to be specific. All of Jesus' prayers were specific. For example, He prayed for "our daily bread" and when Satan requested to sift Peter as wheat, Jesus told Peter, "But I have prayed for you, that your faith should not fail" (Luke 22:32). If you are having problems with your marriage, don't just pray "God bless my marriage," but address the specific areas which need attention, and if you are not sure what those are, make *that* your specific request. If you are concerned about our government, don't just pray for God to direct our leaders, but call them by name and address specific areas and issues such as the Supreme Court's decision on Roe vs. Wade. In each request, be as specific as possible.

A number of times I have been asked if it was okay to pray for healing. James, in chapter five of his epistle, says that we should pray for those who are ill. He expresses it this way:

> Is anyone among you suffering? Let him pray. Is anyone cheerful? Let him sing psalms.

> Is anyone among you sick? Let him call for the elders of the church, and let them pray over him, anointing him with oil in the name of the Lord.

> And the prayer of faith will save the sick, and the Lord will raise him up. And if he has committed sins, he will be forgiven.

> Confess your trespass to one another, and pray for one another, that you may be healed. The effective fervent prayer of a righteous man avails much.

It appears that the sickness would be discussed and prayed for specifically. It also appears that confession may need to be made and those areas of sin prayed for specifically. We are further told to "pray for one another, that you may be healed" (v. 16). Specific requests for healing are proper and should, as the context shows, be accompanied by a time of soul-searching. Spiritual health is, after all, more important than physical health. The praying is done, not only by the sick person (who may not even be able to pray), but specifically by the elders of the church who are called for that purpose. As James says, "let them pray over him, anointing him with oil in the name of the Lord" (v. 14b). Others too, of course, may certainly pray as they become aware of the need.

It may seem that, in considering *what* to pray for, all could be summed up under the topic of "requests." This is such a broad category as to lend itself to that idea. There are, however, two other items which must be examined. We need to pray for God's wisdom and God's will.

That which we so greatly need and that which so easily escapes us in trials is wisdom. James begins his letter by talking of trials. The first thing he says we should ask for is wisdom (James 1:5). Our human or natural wisdom, no matter how great in the world's estimation, is just not equal to the task (1 Cor. 2:6–16). We need that wisdom from above, which only God can give and which only believers can receive.

The basic meaning of "wisdom" in the Old Testament is "skill." It is applied to skill in workmanship in such passages as Exodus 31:1–6 and 35:10. Even then the source of this skill is God. As used in Proverbs, which gives the most exhaustive treatment of wisdom, the idea is clearly that of "skill for living." At all times, but most crucially in a time of trial, we need skill for living; we need God's wisdom.

When we find ourselves in a trial, the first item to take inventory of is wisdom. If we sense a deficiency in this area, it must be cared for immediately by prayer. As James instructed: "If any of you lack wisdom, let him ask of God, who gives to all liberally and without reproach, and it will be given to Him" (James 1:5). God, "who gives to all liberally," is not stingy with His wisdom. He has an abundant supply and will grant us all we need. Neither will He get onto us for asking, but will give "without reproach." The verse even ends with a promise: "and it will be given to him."

Why is it that one person can pray for wisdom and receive it while another person says the same prayer and comes up empty? We have already seen that it is not because God has a lack of supply or lack of desire to give us wisdom. The problem, James goes on to explain, has to do with the faith of the one praying. If you don't believe God will or can grant you wisdom, you will not receive it (James 1:6–7). In fact, since such a person is double-minded, he will prove to be "unstable in all his ways" (James 1:8). It is only the hand of faith that receives wisdom from God.

We also need to subject all of our requests, plans, and desires to the will of God. Above all, what we should want is God's will to be perfectly worked out in our lives. Our will may be corrupted by self-centeredness or misdirected by insufficient knowledge. God's will is always perfect and is always best for us. It is okay to make plans and it is right to pray for specific goals, needs and requests, but as James writes, all of these need to pass the test of God's will.

> Come now, you who say, "Today or tomorrow we will go to such and such a city, spend a year there, buy and sell, and make a profit,"
>
> Whereas you do not know what will happen tomorrow. For what is your life? It is even a vapor that appears for a little time and then vanishes away.
>
> Instead you ought to say, "If the Lord wills, we shall live and do this or that."
>
> (James 4:13–15)

Since even our next breath will be taken only in accordance with God's mercy and will, surely all else that we do must meet the same requirements.

When considering what specifically to pray for, there is nothing better and nothing more urgent than God's will. We should ask for His will to be done in our lives and our circumstances. Having done that, we should seek His wisdom that we might know how to proceed. We should be open to His leading and faithful to follow.

We cannot always be certain of God's will. That there is an element of uncertainty is indicated in James 4:15 when he says "if the Lord wills, we shall live and do this or that." Is it the Lord's will for you to be alive tomorrow? You will know the answer to that question only when tomorrow is over. The goal is not always to know God's will, but to trust that God has a will concerning us and to pray that His will would have precedence over ours. Thus Jesus prayed in the garden "not My will, but Yours, be done" (Luke 22:42). Jesus knew it was the Father's will for Him to go to the cross (John 12:27), but even in those cases where we are not sure of the Father's will, we should pray that it would be accomplished.

There are a number of areas where God has already indicated His will in His Word. We should have no doubt about sinful acts; we don't have to ask God if it is within His will for us to do them. If we would subject all that we do or want to do to the scrutiny of God's Word, many pitfalls would be avoided.

In those cases where we can know God's will, we should both know and do it (James 1:22–25). In those cases where we are not certain, we should subject our plans and ourselves to His will, praying and believing that it will be done (James 4:15).

Prayer is always needed. There is an old Dennis the Menace cartoon that shows Dennis coming out of church. The minister bends down to ask "Do you say a prayer before you eat?" Dennis replies: "Don't have to, my mom's a good cook." We might not always see the need for prayer and that in itself can lead to our woes. Prayer is not optional, it is vital and it is powerful.

A great preacher of the fourth century, John Chrysostom, is credited with the following statement on the power of prayer.

> The potency of prayer hath subdued the strength of fire; it hath bridled the rage of lions, hushed anarchy to rest, extinguished wars, appeased the elements, expelled demons, burst the chains of death, expanded the gates of heaven, assuaged diseases, repelled frauds, rescued cities from destruction, stayed the sun in its course, and arrested the progress of the thunderbolt. Prayer is an all-sufficient panoply, a treasure undiminished, a mine which is never exhausted, a sky unobscured by clouds, a heaven unruffled by storm. It is the root, the fountain, the mother of a thousand blessings.[8]

Instead of giving up in despair that "all we can do is pray," we should rather rejoice in the privilege and power of prayer. Adversity is no match for prayer.

Trials make the promise sweet;
Trials give new life to prayer;
Trials bring me to His feet,
Lay me low, and keep me there

—Charles Spurgeon

WE NEED TO TRUST

I woke up with bandages over my eyes and wrapped around my head. I was six years old and had just had surgery on my eyes to correct a problem. I had no idea where I was, except that I was in a hospital. I could sense it was a large room, for there seemed to be a number of other children coughing, crying, talking, and so forth. I wasn't sure if it was day or night. One thing I was sure of—I had to go to the bathroom! I called out for help and a nurse finally came to my rescue. I explained my problem with the urgency and lack of delicacy common in six-year-old boys. The nurse explained that she would lead me to the bathroom. She would take my hand and guide my steps. As soon as my feet hit the floor I realized how completely disoriented I was. I was scared. I imagined poles in front of me, bed posts to stub my toes on and shoes to trip me up. I complained "I can't see." "*I know* you can't see," the nurse replied, "that's why I'm leading you." Each step was more frightening. "No," I cried, "I can't see!" "Trust me," reassured the nurse. "But you don't understand," I protested, "I don't know where anything is or isn't. I can't see." Her answer was unforgettable. She calmly said: "If you could see, you wouldn't need to trust me."

We need to trust God because He sees what we cannot see; He knows what we may never know. Trusting God means to walk by faith and not by sight (2 Cor. 5:7).

I needed to trust that nurse because I could not see and she could. I probably would never have found that bathroom by myself—certainly not before my bladder gave out. I was hindered from seeing and was forced to rely upon someone else who was not hindered. I had to trust both that she could see and that she would lead me safely through the obstacles. If I could have seen just a little, perhaps by a slit in my bandages, I wonder if I would have tried to make it on my own. That seems to be my natural tendency.

One of our problems as believers is that, even though we know we should walk by faith, we really would much rather walk by sight. Even if we can only see just a little bit, we find it more appealing to follow what we think we know rather than to trust for what we cannot see. To really trust is one of the hardest things we will ever do. It goes against our survival instincts. It means putting our lives into someone else's hands. It means being vulnerable. We feel that if we maintain some small measure of control we can keep hold of *something*—even if we lose. But if someone else is in control we may lose everything. Most of us are not willing to gamble to that degree.

A certain man was walking along a narrow mountain path, not paying close enough attention to where he was going. Suddenly, he slipped over the edge of a cliff. As he fell, he grabbed onto a branch which was growing out of the side of the cliff. Realizing that he could not hold on forever, he called for help:

Man: "Is anybody up there?"
Voice: "Yes, I'm here."
Man: "Great! Who's that?"
Voice: "The Lord."
Man: "Lord, help me!"
Voice: "Do you *trust* me?"
Man: "Yes, I trust you."
Voice: "How *much* do you trust me?"
Man: "I trust you *completely*, Lord."
Voice: "Good, let go of the branch."
Man: "What???"
Voice: "I said, let go of the branch."
Man: (after a long pause) "Is anybody else up there?"

This story is too often typical of our unwillingness to trust. We feel safer trying to hang onto something than letting go and casting ourselves completely into God's care. We do not realize that actually the safest and best course of action is not to rely on self, but to trust in God. We may even seek for "anybody else up there" who could help us without our having to trust or give up what little control we have. We are at times like the Israelites to whom God said: "In returning and rest you shall be saved; in quietness and confidence shall be your strength. But you would not, and you said, 'No, for we shall flee on horses'—therefore you shall flee!" (Isaiah 30:15–16).

Real peace comes only with genuine trust. If you have a lack of peace, it would be good to examine your level of trust. Numerous times the Lord promises peace to those who trust in Him. A personal favorite is Isaiah 26:3 which says: "You will keep him in perfect peace, whose mind is stayed on You, because he trusts in You." That's the kind of peace the world knows nothing of. It is unavailable to those who do not trust. We, who are children of God by His grace, have the privilege of trusting God and finding in that trust perfect peace.

Kyle Gibson, a dear brother in the Lord, will be ninety-one this year. He loves to speak of the faithfulness of God. His has not been an easy life by any means. He has gone through just about everything you can imagine. His favorite Bible character is Job and he quotes from that book quite often. One of his oft-quoted verses is, "Man who is born of woman is of few days and full of trouble" (Job 14:1). He knows what it means to live a life full of problems. But Kyle's testimony does not end there. He hastens on to add that God is faithful and gracious to see us through every trial. He beams with confidence that God will never leave or forsake us and He will be with us until we go to be with Him. Kyle loves to say with Job: "Though He slay me, yet will I trust Him" (Job 13:15). When I see such a fellow-soldier of Christ who has gone through the battles and has claimed victory in Jesus, it makes me want to join the ranks with Kyle and Job and a host of others who will proclaim to God's glory, "though He slay me, yet will I trust Him!" Why not join in today? There is great peace in real trust.

Trust, as we have seen, is not our natural inclination. Even for seasoned veterans of the faith there may be times when the trials seem to so overshadow our trust as to leave us in despair. Trust is not cheap; it is not easily come by. It is easy to just say "trust"; it is quite another thing to achieve it. Distrust seems much more natural to our humanness. I would not be surprised to learn that Eve counted Adam's ribs every night when he got home!

The Apostle Paul is viewed, and rightly so, as a great example of faith and trust. He never seemed to falter or stumble in his walk; he never seemed to waiver in his trust. He was able to say as his life drew to a close: "I have fought the good fight, I have finished the race, I have kept the faith" (2 Tim. 4:7). But does that mean Paul never knew despair? No, Paul knew despair, but he also found the way of escape.

There is a short and intriguing insight into Paul's life in Second Corinthians. We find there this account:

> For we do not want you to be ignorant, brethren, of our trouble which came to us in Asia: that we were burdened beyond measure, above strength, so that we despaired even of life.

> Yes we had the sentence of death in ourselves, that we should not trust in ourselves but in God who raises the dead, who delivered us from so great a death, and does deliver us; in whom we trust that He will still deliver us.

What the exact nature of Paul's trouble was we are not told. Paul designates the place as Asia, and perhaps the Corinthian church would have known from that identification the specific problem he spoke of. At any rate, it is not crucial for us to know (or we would have been told!) and our focus is brought rather to the depth of his turmoil.

Paul is quite frank about his emotional state. He says: "we were burdened beyond measure, above strength, so that we despaired even of life." His emotional upheaval could not be calculated or measured. It went off the scale. There was no way he could take anymore. The nature of this trial proved to be above his strength. Worst of all, he saw no hope, no ending of the trial, no lessening of the affliction. It was so severe that this giant of the faith "despaired even of life." If you have wondered if you were the only one who ever felt that way, take comfort, for we who have known despair make up the majority! Our comfort, of course, comes, not because we are in the same boat, but because we have the same Captain Who will see us through the storm.

Paul goes on to say: "Yes, we had the sentence of death in ourselves." After this last note of despair he adds the purpose and the song of hope: "that we should not trust in ourselves, but in God Who raises the dead." Paul realized that he was burdened beyond *his* measure and above *his* strength. His despair was that *he* could do nothing to change the situation. God lets us get to the end of our rope so that He is all we have left to cling to. Paul communicates that by the purpose clause "that we should not trust in ourselves but in God who raises the dead." We have no reason to trust in ourselves. We have but puny strength and limited vision. God's strength never fails and His vision is perfect. We can and we must trust Him. He will safely lead us.

Paul looked back at the situation and testified that God "delivered us from so great a death" (past tense); he looked at his present circumstances and, realizing the same God is watching and working, was able to say "and does deliver us" (present tense); he looked toward the future with the eye of faith to proclaim "that He will still deliver us" (future tense). He Who calls us to cast all of our cares upon Him is worthy of our trust. When we trust God for today, one day at a time, He takes care of all of our tomorrows. An unknown poet expressed it this way:

> *Build a little fence of trust*
> *around today;*
> *Fill the space with loving work*
> *and therein stay,*
> *Look not through the sheltering bars*
> *upon tomorrow;*
> *God will help you bear what comes*
> *of joy or sorrow*

What does it mean to trust? Let's think of it in relationship to a friend. If your best friend called and said he would come over this evening, would you believe him? That is trust. When he came over, could you trust him with a secret? Let's say you had a million dollars you needed someone to hold for you, could you hand it to your friend without worrying if he would buy airline tickets for parts unknown the next day? If you could, that's trust. God is much more reliable than your friend. An unavoidable accident or conflict may come up to prevent your friend from coming over. There are no accidents with God, no unforeseen conflicts and no complications which could prevent Him from doing exactly what He has promised. Your friend might let your secret slip (without realizing it, of course) or he might leave the country quickly (he was planning a trip to Tibet anyway), but God will never let you down or slip up. If you can trust your friend, who is a sinner, can you not all the more trust a holy God? If you believe your friend will be faithful to his word, do you not also believe that righteous God, Who cannot lie (Titus 1:2), will absolutely and completely keep every promise He has made?

It is a blessed thing to trust in God and to find Him faithful. It is a blessed thing, but it is not always easy and it is never neutral. It requires walking by faith *because* we cannot see.

> Nothing before, nothing behind;
> The steps of faith
> Fall on the seeming void, and find
> The Rock beneath
> John Greenleaf Whittier

WE NEED TO BE CONTENT IN WHATEVER SITUATION WE ARE IN

It is not too hard to be content in a situation where things are going reasonably well. The challenge comes when our situation is altered and we find ourselves in a trial, suffering, facing adversity, a victim. We naturally prefer things to stay the same (if they are good!) and we are not at all content when they change for the worse.

Our problem is one of focus. Our attention becomes riveted to what has changed instead of what remains the same. We agonize over the cursings and forget to count the blessings. We see the storm more clearly than we see the Savior, and like Peter, we begin to sink. Contentment concentrates on present provision and what has not changed; discontentment concentrates on what was lost or what might be lost and longs for that which has changed.

One evening Jesus and His disciples were crossing the sea in a boat. A storm arose and the waves beat against the boat and it began to fill with water. The disciples were naturally concerned, to say the least, in this change of weather. They believed they were in danger of perishing and could not understand why Jesus was not at their side bailing out water as fast as He could. They found Him, we can be sure to their utter amazement, in the stern asleep! They awakened Him and asked: "Teacher, do you not care that we are perishing?" The story, as recorded in Mark 4:39–40, continues as follows:

Then He arose and rebuked the wind, and said to the sea, "Peace, be still!" And the wind ceased and there was a great calm.

But He said to them, "Why are you so fearful? How is it that you have no faith?"

Jesus obviously had a different focus or perspective of the situation than did the disciples. He asked them *why* they were so afraid, meaning, of course, that they should not have been. He pointed to their lack of faith as the problem. If there had been no storm, if things had not changed, the disciples would not have feared. They were afraid because of what had changed in their situation. Their focus was on the storm, the problem, and not on those things which were steadfast and unshakable.

What were some of the things that remained unchanged? The power and sovereignty of God were not affected. In fact, Jesus immediately displayed both. God's love and care for them were undiminished. God's purpose for them and for His Son was not blown about by the winds of change. Jesus had a destiny with the cross and He knew that. The most violent storm in the world could not have deterred God's will or stayed His hand. The disciples did not realize that they were in the safest spot in the whole world! The Titanic was thought to be unsinkable; this tiny vessel truly was. There were more and greater things which had *not* changed than had changed. The house that is built on sand will fall when a storm comes because it is founded on something that changes. The house that is built on the rock will remain steadfast through the storm because it is founded on that which does not change. Where is our focus—on that which changes or on that which is unchangeable?

We need to apply this thinking to ourselves in times of adversity. When our situation takes a change for the worse, we must force ourselves to focus on what has not changed, especially in reference to God and His faithfulness. We can also be grateful for such things as the Word which never changes, for the hope that is laid up for us, those brothers and sisters in Christ who stand by us, and even for secular items such as employment.

Being content in whatever situation we are in is not a natural trait, but rather an acquired attitude. It is something which may be learned. Paul wrote to the Philippians:

But I rejoiced in the Lord greatly that now at last your care of me has flourished again: though you surely did care, but you lacked opportunity.

Not that I speak in regard to need, for I have learned in whatever state I am, to be content:

I know how to be abased, and I know how to abound. Everywhere and in all things I have learned both to be full and to be hungry, both to abound and to suffer need.

I can do all things through Christ who strengthens me.
(Philippians 3:10–13)

Paul was grateful that the Philippians had demonstrated their care for him by meeting his physical needs. He realized and assured them that he knew their care was constant. They had not given only because they had not had the opportunity. He does not want to negate their gift, but at the same time he desires to teach them a spiritual lesson he himself had learned, namely, contentment. He had evidently been in need, as far as the world's standards are concerned, but he insists: "not that I speak in regard to need . . ." Paul had learned to be content in any situation. Paul could have made it without their gift. He was thankful for their gift, but more because of their ability and willingness to give (plus the spiritual fruit abounding to their account – vs 17) than his opportunity to receive. We should seek to meet one another's needs (James 2:15–16).

But when we are on the receiving end, what should be our attitude, whether others meet our needs or not? Paul says it should be contentment. In the end, it is God who supplies all of our needs anyway (v. 19).

Paul said: "I have learned in whatever state I am, to be content." He knew that even if situations changed (abased . . . abound, to be full and to be hungry, etc.) he could always rely upon the Lord. It was with that thought in mind that Paul wrote the often quoted and sometimes misapplied verse thirteen: "I can do all things through Christ who strengthens me." The "all things" which Paul was referring to has its direct application in the preceding verse. He meant specifically that whether things were going well or terrible, whether he was hungry or full, whether his situation changed or remained the same, Christ strengthened him and enabled him to not only endure, but actually to be content.

Contentment has its roots in the steadfast nature of our Lord. It is only "through Christ" that we can "do all things." Contentment is a lesson which can be learned only in the school of faith.

Paul wrote to Timothy that "godliness with contentment is great gain" (1 Tim. 6:6). It is hard to imagine one without the other. A truly godly person would have his mind set "on things above, not on things on the earth" (Colossians 3:2). He would be actively seeking the kingdom of God and His righteousness as a first priority (Matthew 6:33). He would take to heart the command: "You shall love the Lord your God with all your heart, with all your soul, and with all your might" (Deuteronomy 6:5). Show me a person who is doing that and I will show you a content believer.

Conversely, a person who is truly content in any situation is so because of the kind of godliness described above. Man is either self-seeking or God-seeking. Either his treasure is buried in the earth or in heaven. The things of earth are not always available; they are never in sufficient quantity to satisfy, and they last but for a season. The things of heaven, by contrast, are always available; they cause our cup to run over and they abide forever. A person who is content has found the source of contentment in godliness.

I read of a tremendous example of "godliness with contentment" in "Our Daily Bread" in a devotion written by Henry G. Bosch. The story runs as follows:

In her girlhood, Hanna R. Higgins of Australia suffered from a very serious and baffling bone disease. As the ailment progressed, she lost the use of her legs, and finally they had to be amputated. Bedridden for more than 50 years, she endured intense suffering yet bore it with Christian patience. In fact, her life was a benediction to all who came in contact with her. Being well "established in the faith," she abounded "with thanksgiving" and showed to everyone that a believer can be happy even in the most depressing and painful circumstances.

In her book "Cloud and Sunshine," written when she was 77, she said, "I long for all to prove as I do, that with our loving Saviour's help it is possible to be happy under very trying conditions." She learned to rejoice in the Lord, and she called her sickroom "Thanksgiving Corner." As people visited her, they sensed God's presence in a special way and always left uplifted and blessed. She wrote notes of cheer and encouragement to people all over the world. More than 200 missionaries were on her prayer list, and she undergirded them with almost unceasing intercession at the Throne of Grace. Handicapped though she was, she sent each of them at least one letter of comfort and help every year.

May we learn as Paul did and as Hanna did that "it is possible to be happy under very trying conditions!"

In closing, it is necessary to correct a possible misunderstanding of all that has been said. Being content in a situation does not mean that we should not seek to change it. For example, Jesus calmed the storm. As we shall discuss in a later chapter, the Lord expects us to do what we can and to use the good sense He has given us. If we are sick, we should see a doctor, take medicine, etc. If we are out of work, we should seek employment. Being content does not remove our responsibility. We are to do what we can and should, all the while focusing our attention on the Savior.

WE NEED TO BE PATIENT

Snap went the mousetrap on my probing finger. I thought the incident was a rather painful one and wasted no time in rescuing my finger from its captor. A shrill note was also heard emitting immediately from my mouth. Pain destroys patience. There was no way that I was going to stroll over to my wife in the other room and ask her to kindly remove the mousetrap from my throbbing appendage if she had the time! Our reaction to pain is immediate.

As will be explained in a later chapter, the Lord expects us to do what we can, like removing the mousetrap from our finger. But what happens in those numerous cases where we cannot remove the pain or its source? What happens when our only option is to endure? We learn in a deeper way the value of prayer and the lesson of patience.

Paul wrote that our bodies should be presented to God as "a living sacrifice, holy, acceptable unto God . . ." (Romans 12:1). He then went on to describe some elements in our life and life-style which should indicate whether we have indeed made such a sacrifice. Within that list we find the following three elements: "rejoicing in hope, patient in tribulation, continuing steadfast in prayer" (Romans 12:12). If we have presented our bodies as a living, holy sacrifice to God, as the Lord exhorts us through the Apostle Paul to do, then we will be, among other things, patient in tribulation. The other side of that coin may not be pleasant to see (but we must), for it tells us that if we find ourselves impatient in tribulation, we must seriously question the degree to which we have been obedient in offering ourselves to God. This is *not* a question of salvation, but rather consecration. We are living proof that it is possible for believers to be less than 100% consecrated to God. Whatever percent is *not* consecrated constitutes sin. Further, the less consecrated to God we are, the less we will see these elements and evidences, such as patience, in our lives.

We all have varying degrees of patience or, closer to the mark, impatience. It seems that we have too readily accepted that fact and conceded the battle. Patience is viewed as a luxury—something we would like to have but can't or won't pay the price for. It is something we admire in others, demand of our children, and weakly hope for ourselves. Patience is something we need toward the driver of the car in front of us and hope for from the driver behind us. Patience is viewed as being valuable yet not as being pursued. It is like gold shining out of a rock wall—beautiful and precious, but only those who go through all the labor and effort and time to possess it will profit from it. The rest just admire it and wish they had more of it.

The Bible paints a different picture. Patience is not a luxury or an option; it is expected of every believer. All of us who name Jesus as our Lord should be "patient in tribulation." Since not one of us is perfect, all of us lack complete patience to some degree. The point is, that lack should not be seen as a luxury but as a problem, not as an option but as sin. Lack of patience betrays a lack of trust. We call upon the Lord in our tribulation but then respond as if we were not quite sure whether He will answer. This is especially a problem when His timing does not correspond with ours. To say that we are trusting God with our problem and then be impatient for the solution is a contradiction.

The Greek word in our New Testament translated as "patience" is formed by putting the word *hupo*, which means "under," together with the word *meno*, which means "to abide." Patience literally means "to abide under." Our first reaction in tribulation is to get out from under whatever is weighing us down. That is not a wrong response (remember the mousetrap) but it may not be what the Lord has in store for us. Our Father may desire for us "to abide under" the tribulation for a time.

In my teen years I used to lift weights in training for football. At the beginning of one particular summer I started out pressing just 75 pounds. I could handle that amount for short periods of time. By the end of summer I could lift twice that amount and could hold the 75 pounds in the air for quite awhile. The more I exercised the stronger I became and the longer I could "abide under" the weight. How long you can abide under the weight of tribulation is a good indication of the strength of your patience. If your patience needs more strengthening, the Lord may send you the proper amount of weight (or wait!) in order to exercise your trust and build up your patience (see Romans 5:3–5). The Lord does not teach us patience to punish us, but to help us. Think about it; are you at peace when you are impatient? If we are to really know the peace that can be ours, it must come through the lesson of patience. Since our Lord wants to give us His kind of peace, He works in our life to bring it about. The peace which He gives in tribulation comes from knowing Him and trusting Him. That is why Jesus said, "These things I have spoken to you, that in Me you may have peace. In the world you will have tribulation but be of good cheer, I have overcome the world" (John 16:33). Patience means abiding under the problem and trusting the Lord's provision all the while. Peace results from that kind of patience.

Victory is found not in fleeing, but in remaining steadfast on the Rock. A good soldier is not one who flees but one who is faithful. We are not always to escape but we are often to endure.

I have sometimes found that the answer to my problem comes in the very process of patience and perseverance. One writer has expressed that idea in a humorous way:

Two frogs fell into a can of cream
    Or so I've heard it told
The sides of the can were shiny and steep,
    The cream was deep and cold.
"O what's the use" croaked No. one,
    'Tis fate; no help around.
Goodbye my friends, Goodbye sad world!"
    And weeping still he drowned.
But No. two, of sterner stuff

Dog paddled in surprise
The while he wiped his creamy face
   And dried his creamy eyes.
"I'll swim awhile, at least," he said—
   Or so I've heard he said;
"It really wouldn't help the world
   If one more frog were dead."
An hour or two he kicked and swam,
   Not once he stopped to mutter,
But kicked and kicked and swam and kicked,
   Then hopped out, via butter!

T. C. Hamlet

Sometimes, as mentioned above, the act of persevering in patience will lead to the answer we are seeking. There are other times, however (and they seem more numerous to me), when the object of our tribulation is to cause us to see God's grace and deliverance and not our own. It is only by being still and being patient that we can see and appreciate God's hand. Imagine trying to look into a microscope or telescope and jumping around at the same time. There are wonders to behold, but only by those who are still. The Lord instructs us: "Be still, and know that I am God; I will be exalted among the nations, I will be exalted in the earth!" (Psalm 46:10). God continually proves who He is—are you still enough to see it? When we are still and wait on the Lord for His perfect working, then we can testify of the great things He has done and God is thereby "exalted in the earth."

If patience were easy, there would not be a need for this chapter. The truth is, it is difficult to stay still. Put a two- or three-year-old child on a stool and watch how long he remains still (no ropes allowed)! One must cultivate the ability to remain still. Our natural inclination is to get out from under our problem as quickly and painlessly as possible. Consider the following story by David McCasland:[9]

Her car was stalled at the intersection, the hood was up, and she flagged me down to help.

"I can't get it started," she said. "But if you jiggle the wire on the battery, I think it will work."

126

I grabbed the positive battery cable and it came off in my hand. Definitely too loose.

"The terminal needs to be tightened up," I told her. "I can fix it if you have some tools."

"My husband says to just jiggle the wire," she replied. "It always works. Why don't you try that?"

I paused a moment, wondering why her husband didn't ride around town with her so he would be available when the wire needed jiggling.

Finally I said, "Ma'am, if I jiggle the wire, you're going to need someone else to do it every time you shut the engine off. If you'll give me two minutes and a wrench, we can solve the problem and you can forget about it.

Reluctantly, she fumbled under the front seat and then extended a crescent wrench through the window of the old car. As I tightened the battery terminal, it occurred to me how many times I try to get the "quick fix" from God.

"I have this problem, Lord, and if You'll just jiggle the wire, things will be OK. I'm in a hurry, so let's just get me going again the quickest way possible."

But God doesn't want to "jiggle the wire." He wants to take the time necessary to deal with my real problem and fix it.

To get the long-term solution to the pressing needs in my life requires a complete surrender to God and a willingness to proceed on His terms. I must cooperate with Him in whatever it takes for as long as it takes.

That dear lady in the car could have waved me off, kept her crescent wrench hidden, and looked for someone else to provide the quick fix. Instead, she was willing to wait.

As she drove away with her tightened terminal, I asked the Lord to say "No!" the next time I want Him to jiggle a wire for me.

Instead of looking for a "quick fix" from God, we should be seeking His perfect will to be completely worked out in our lives. That makes patience necessary, but not necessarily easy. Paul, recognizing both the need and the problem, wrote to the new converts at Colosse:

> For this reason we also, since the day we heard it, do not cease to pray for you, and to ask that you may be filled with the knowledge of His will in all wisdom and spiritual understanding: that you may have a walk worthy of the Lord, fully pleasing Him, being fruitful in every good work and increasing in the knowledge of God: strengthened with all might, according to His glorious power, for all patience and long-suffering with joy;
>
> (Colossians 1:9–11)

We cannot be patient in our own strength. We know from painful experience that our natural patience is shorter than a hair on a fly's leg. We need God's strength to be patient and so Paul prays that the believers might be "strengthened with all might according to His glorious power." The reason for this supernatural strength is "for (or unto) all patience and longsuffering with joy."

By God's enablement we can be strengthened to be patient, to abide under, to be still in order that we may experience God's working and be, in turn, strengthened through the process and by the process. Every believer has the capacity for patience. God's strength is the door; trust is the key.

WE NEED TO BE STEADFAST

Adversity should draw us closer to God. Trials should cause us to run to the Father and cling to Him like a vine clings to a tree during a storm. Suffering should bring us to the Great Physician. Sorrows should lead us to the Man of Sorrows. Wounded sheep should seek the care of the Great Shepherd. But often the opposite happens. Sometimes we run *from* God instead of *to* God. When that happens, our situation only worsens. Why then would we do such a thing? I suppose there are a number of plausible answers to that question. Two key reasons are: (1) our sinful response of anger toward God and (2) Satan's deceitful strategy to move us away from God.

Anger is a reaction to someone or something which is disagreeable to us. God displays anger at unrighteousness. It has been well suggested that man's anger is a kind of righteous indignation in his own eyes.[10] The key, of course, is the phrase "in his own eyes." Since God has perfect vision, knowledge and understanding, His indignation must be truly just at all times. Man, on the other hand, has blurred vision, limited knowledge and inadequate understanding. Add to these limitations the presence of a sin nature and it becomes readily apparent why man's anger is seldom righteous! Man's anger is *never* righteous when it is directed against God.

All too often I have heard people blame God for their troubles. Usually it is indicated in questions such as: "Why did God take my wife from me?" "Why did God let my husband leave me?" "How could God allow my child to be born with this handicap?" "How could God let me lose my job?" "How long is God going to wait before He finally does something about _____?" "Why doesn't God answer my prayers?" "Doesn't God realize how much I have already gone through?"

These kinds of questions reflect a frustration vented at God. There is a thinly veiled shaking of the fist at God revealed by the complainant. There is an underlying questioning of God's goodness, mercy, power, knowledge, wisdom, concern, provision, justice, and sovereignty. Serious accusations from puny man to a perfect God! I have also found there to be, without exception, a distinct lack of trust on the part of the questioner. The less trust, the more questions there are. What has really caused the person to move from God is not the adversity, but their lack of trust. First comes the problem, then because of lack of trust, questions arise.

There are many times when someone's initial reaction to suffering is to question God. That does not necessarily reflect a lack of trust. Upon further reflection the believer realizes that God is still perfect and that even if the situation is unexplainable, God knows. The problem comes when the individual persists in questioning and, in reality, demanding from God an account of His actions. "But indeed, O man, who are you to reply against God? Will the thing formed say to him who formed it, "why have you made me like this?" Does not the potter have power over the clay . . . ?" (Romans 9:20–21)

We need to be steadfast. The worst thing to do in an adverse situation is to move away from the One who offers our best, if not our only, hope. To respond in anger and refuse to speak to Him (like we do to one another) or to refuse to hear from Him by ignoring His Word, is like an army in need of supplies blowing up its own bridges.

The frustration, hurt, and uncertainty which are revealed in an attitude of anger toward God need to be dealt with individually. The anger is just a sign that something else is wrong. Lay before the Lord your problem of frustration, the hurt that you feel, and the uncertainty that plagues you. Recognize that anger toward God is not only sin, it is silly.

When I went to Grace Seminary the second time, I did so with less finances than the first time around. I had seen, however, a job offer from a local company as an "open door" to enable our move back to Indiana. Soon after moving, the company informed me that, due to a policy change, the position had to be filled from within the company. No job. No problem—God will supply another one. Except He didn't. Days passed. Weeks passed with no income. Everything we had was gone. I remember telling God "I can't take one more day without getting a job!" The next day came and went—still no job. I felt abandoned by God. I would have packed up my wife and three children and moved, except that God had not left me enough money to do so. I questioned my decision to move in the first place. I questioned my ability to know God's will. I questioned the provision of God. But I did not question my own sinful heart or what God's purpose might have been. I felt He was doing nothing.

Then a friend asked me to fill a pulpit. I did so, especially since it paid. I began to speak in various churches, some of which were looking for a pastor. Now I had decided that, for personal reasons, I would *not* pastor a church while in Seminary. I had looked everywhere for a position, except in the ministry. I had, in effect, told God that I would not do the one thing which He had called me to do. Confessing this sin brought great relief. I was soon called to pastor a very gracious rural congregation. My need for income was met by the *place* where God wanted me to be. It was my rebelliousness and not God's lack of care which was the root of my problem. God used this episode to teach me both obedience and patience.

We also need to be steadfast because of Satan's deceitful strategy to move us away from God. Satan uses suffering and adversity as tools to shake our faith. When God pointed out the faithfulness of Job to Satan, Satan responded with attacks on Job's family, possessions, relationships, and health in order to move him away from his faith in God. Job was steadfast and Satan lost.

Satan and his cohorts will attack us as well and with the same purpose—to try to shake our faith and move us from God. Paul, recognizing the nature of the battle, wrote to the Ephesians:

Finally, my brethren, be strong in the Lord and in the power of His might. Put on the whole armor of God, that you may be able to stand against the wiles of the devil. For we do not wrestle against flesh and blood, but against principalities, against powers, against the rulers of the darkness of this age, against spiritual hosts of wickedness in the heavenly places. Therefore take up the whole armor of God, that you may be able to withstand in the evil day, and having done all, to stand.

(Ephesians 6:10–13)

The key to defeating Satan is to keep standing, to remain steadfast. We have to be strong to do that. Our own strength is not enough. Even an archangel's strength is not equal to the task (Jude 9). We need supernatural strength, and so Paul says "be strong in the Lord and in the power of His might." In our own strength we fall; in God's strength we stand. Just as an electric lamp must be plugged into a power source to emit any light, so we must be plugged into our power source, God, to be able to do anything at all (John 15:5).

The power to resist the devil depends on our closeness to God (James 4:7–8). The closer we are to God, the less influence Satan will have in moving us away. As we move away from God, however, we disconnect from our power source and we become easy targets for Satan.

We are enabled to stand fast by the power of God and by the armor of God. Paul says to put *all* the armor on. Neglecting any part of the armor makes us vulnerable at that point. A knight going out to battle without his shield would be foolish and soon defeated, even if he did have his helmet, breastplate, etc. The armor which God supplies is listed by Paul in the following manner:

Stand therefore, having girded your waist with *truth*, having put on the breastplate of *righteousness*, and having shod your feet with the preparation of *the gospel of peace*, above all, taking the shield of *faith* with which you will be able to quench all the fiery darts of the wicked one. And take the helmet of *salvation*, and the sword of the Spirit, which is the *word of God*; *praying* always with all prayer and supplication in the Spirit, being watchful to this end with all perseverance and supplication for all the saints.

(Ephesians 6:14–18)

The purpose of the armor is given in verse thirteen: ". . . that you may be able to withstand in the evil day, and having done all, to stand." Satan wants to move us; God wants us to stand. Whether we move or stand depends on whose power we are living by and whose armor we are fighting in.

We wrestle not against flesh and blood,
But against the rulers of sin,
And whether we stand or whether we fall
In the midst of life's battle din,
Depends on the armor we choose to wear
And whether we trust in Him.

He does not ask that we take by siege
The evil in places high,
Nor does he expect we surrender all
To the forces of evil night,
But "Stand" says He, "in the evil day
Thy needs I shall supply."

Stand with your loins all girded by truth,
Your heart protected by right,
Prepared to go with the gospel of peace
Where neither is Hope nor Light,
Though the wiles of the devil are subtle and dark,
We walk by faith, not sight.

The enemy hurls his darts of doubt
To question our rank and role,
And the sneer of scorn will seek its mark
Straight to our feeble soul,
But the shield of faith rebukes the sting
As we march to eternity's goal

The plan of salvation our helmet is,
Assuring us heaven's reward,
His Word and the Spirit defends our hopes
With strength as a mighty sword,

Our duty we seek through the order of prayer,
But *victory* comes from the *Lord*.

Alma Barkman

We can only stand fast when we realize we are in a spiritual battle and we rely on spiritual weapons and warfare. As Paul wrote to the Corinthians:

> For though we walk in the flesh, we do not war according to the flesh. For the weapons of our warfare are not carnal but mighty in God for pulling down strongholds, casting down arguments and every high thing that exalts itself against the knowledge of God, bringing every thought into captivity to the obedience of Christ.
>
> (2 Corinthians 10:3–5)

We are told to both stand fast *in* the faith (1 Cor. 16:13) and to stand fast *by* faith (2 Cor. 1:24). To stand fast "in the faith" means to cling to the spiritual reality of who God is and what He has said. To stand fast "by faith" means to actively exercise faith, i.e., to believe and trust and to live accordingly. If, for example, I believe God is sovereign and that He has promised to take care of my needs, and if I rest my trust on those facts and live accordingly, I will stand. If I waiver on any point, I will fall. But there is no need or reason to waiver, fall, or be moved. God has been gracious to supply *all* we need to stand and be steadfast.

Those who are steadfast every day will also be steadfast in the day of adversity. Those who cling to the cross will not be dislodged by any storm. Those who stand on the Rock shall not be moved.

WE NEED TO BE JOYFUL

*"We will not dishonor our Bridegroom
by mourning in His presence"*—Charles Spurgeon

As a new believer, when I first heard that a Christian should be joyful even in times of trial, adversity, and suffering, my first response was "you have got to be kidding!" You might try this simple experiment: hit your thumb with a hammer and then calculate your level of joy. It seems like a contradiction at worst and a paradox at best. Only sick minds equate pain with joy.

How then can we account for the clear biblical teaching of joy in trials? In the first place, we are never told that we would receive joy from self-inflicted wounds. Hitting your thumb with a hammer is not designed to bring joy into your life. The same principle holds true for other self-inflicted wounds, especially in the area of personal sin. If your sin causes adversity, which it usually does, do not expect it to be a joyful situation.

Secondly, we are never told to be joyful *because* of the trial or adversity but *in* the trial or adversity. We are not to rejoice because we broke a leg, but we can be joyful even in that circumstance. We are not to rejoice in sin (Eph. 5:11–12) and so we are not expected to be joyful that our spouse left us, for example. That does not mean we cannot have joy *despite* the situation. It only means we will not rejoice *because* of the situation.

The Bible indicates there are at least four reasons why we can be joyful even in times of adversity. Those reasons are: because of our inheritance, because of our identification, because of God's working and because of God's will.

We can be joyful in times of adversity because of our inheritance as believers. The unbeliever does not share this inheritance and misses out on the benefit of joy. Each believer is indwelt by the Holy Spirit (Romans 8:9, 14) and should bear spiritual fruit (John 15:1–8; Matt. 7:15–20). The fruit of the Spirit is listed for us in Galatians 5:22–23. The first fruit listed is love, which is fitting. The very next fruit of the Spirit which should be evident in the life of a believer is "joy."

Notice that joy is not the fruit of the person, but the fruit of the Spirit. Joy is not something in and of ourselves which might be attained by extra effort. Joy is attained and maintained by the presence of and yieldedness to the Holy Spirit. Our level of joy is not so much dependent on the depth of our trials as it is on the depth of our walk with God. As Paul wrote: "If we live in the Spirit, let us also walk in the Spirit" (Gal. 5:25). Those who are walking in the Spirit, i.e., following Him in daily obedience, will find His fruit (including joy) much more abundant. Those who are walking in the Spirit on a continual basis will know what it means to "rejoice always" (2 Thess. 5:16).

We tend to confuse happiness with joy. Happiness is dependent on external circumstances, whereas joy is dependent on internal circumstances. Happiness comes and goes with events depending on how they affect our lives. Joy is abiding regardless of events. Happiness is temporary; joy lasts. Happiness is based on emotion; joy, though felt like an emotion, is based on commitment. Happiness can be found in the life of a believer or a nonbeliever; joy can only be found in a believer. The cost of pursuing happiness is often expensive in more ways than one. Joy, on the other hand, is free (the price having been paid for us) and even pays dividends. Happiness is not always possible; joy is always attainable. When we refer to having joy in times of adversity, we are referring to something beyond happiness; we are referring to the blessing of joy that comes from the hand of God. "For the kingdom of God is not food and drink, but righteousness and peace and joy in the Holy Spirit" (Romans 14:17).

The second reason we can be joyful in times of adversity is because of our identification with Christ. Peter wrote: "Beloved, do not think it strange concerning the fiery trial which is to try you, as though some strange thing happened to you; but rejoice to the extent that you partake of Christ's sufferings, that when His glory is revealed, you may also be glad with exceeding joy" (1 Peter 4:12–13).

We identify first of all with Christ's sufferings. If the world will attack our Lord, we are living in danger also. Persecution is more open in other countries than it is in ours. We should cherish and seek to preserve these freedoms. However, to say there is no persecution against Christians in America is wrong. It may be subtle and at times disguised, like a wolf in sheep's clothing, but it is still real. Would people in the United States attack our Lord? Yes! Blasphemy, anti-biblical statements, anti-Christian remarks, biases and immoral situations are rampant in movies, television, books, and magazines. Any issue of the American Family Association Journal will clearly demonstrate both the trend and the depth of the barrage against the teachings of Christ. If they attack our Lord, we cannot expect to come away unscratched. Jesus told his followers:

> If the world hates you, you know that it hated Me before it hated you. If you were of the world, the world would love its own. Yet because you are not of the world, but I chose you out of the world, therefore the world hates you. Remember the word that I said to you, "A servant is not greater than his master." If they persecuted Me, they will also persecute you. If they kept My word, they will keep yours also.
> (John 15:18–20)

What does this have to do with joy? Our rejoicing is not *because* we are attacked, but the *reason* we are attacked. When the Apostles were arrested, threatened, beaten, and then thrown out, ". . . they departed from the presence of the council, rejoicing that they were counted worthy to suffer shame for His name" (Acts 5:41). To know that we are so closely identified with Jesus ought to make us rejoice!

Our identification with Jesus results in joy, not only because we share in His sufferings, but also because we share in His glory. We do not thereby take away from or diminish His glory anymore than we reduce His sufferings on the cross when we "partake of Christ's sufferings." Rather, because He is glorified, the light of His glory reflects on us too. Peter often connected suffering with glory (see, for example, 1 Peter 4:13, 14, 16). The world may seek to shame us, but the Lord will exalt the humble and lift up the abased and cause His light to shine on us. We are precious to God, His children, and joint heirs with Christ ". . . if indeed we suffer with Him, that we may also be glorified together. For I consider that the sufferings of this present time are not worthy to be compared with the glory which shall be revealed in us" (Romans 8:17–18).

Our identification with Christ leads to our rejoicing *in* Christ. Paul wrote to the Philippians: "Finally, my brethren, rejoice in the Lord. For me to write the same things to you is not tedious, but for you it is safe" (Phil 3:1) Paul was concerned for their spiritual welfare. He did not mind repeating himself in order to make his point, and one of his chief points in this epistle is "Rejoice in the Lord" and as he says yet again later, "Rejoice in the Lord always. Again I will say, rejoice!" (Phil 4:4). Mark carefully that this rejoicing is specifically "in" the *Lord*, not in the circumstance, self, or anyone or anything else. True joy is found in Jesus alone. If you are lacking it, flee to Him!

The third reason we can be joyful in times of adversity is because of God's working. If we suffered through adversity and had nothing to show for it, we might have reason to bemoan the fact. But God uses trials to build character. A familiar passage in this regard is found in James, where we read:

> My brethren, count it all joy when you fall into various trials, knowing that the testing of your faith produces patience. But let patience have its perfect work, that you may be perfect and complete, lacking nothing.
>
> (James 1:2–4)

We should have joy knowing that the Lord cares enough about us to work with us. He does not abandon us to our own resources and character development. He carefully engineers our lives to have the right balance of trials and blessings, like a flower which needs both sunshine and rain, in order that we might grow into something beautiful in His sight.

The Apostle Peter expresses a similar thought in his first letter:

> In this you greatly rejoice, though now for a little while, if need be, you have been grieved by various trials, that the genuineness of your faith, being much more precious than gold that perishes, though it is tested by fire, may be found to praise, honor, and glory at the revelation of Jesus Christ, whom having not seen you love. Though now you do not see Him, yet believing, you rejoice with joy inexpressible and full of glory, receiving the end of your faith—the salvation of your souls.
>
> (1 Peter 1:6–9)

The Lord tests the "genuineness of your faith" because it is "much more precious than gold that perishes." He does so, not in order that He might know, but that we might know. We rejoice in that the Lord continues to work in and with us because it is a demonstration of His continual care and concern for our spiritual health. We are precious in His sight and our trials are to Him like gold under fire.

The fourth reason why we can be joyful in times of adversity is because of God's will. Since our God is sovereign, we know that nothing, including adversity, comes our way without first having passed through His hands. Knowing that, we should "run with endurance the race that is set before us" (Heb. 12:1). One of the most amazing verses in the Bible follows that statement. We go on to read: "Looking unto Jesus, the author and finisher of our faith, who for the joy that was set before Him endured the cross, despising the shame, and has sat down at the right hand of the throne of God" (Heb. 12:2). It is awe-inspiring to read that Jesus viewed the cross as "the joy that was set before Him." In what way could it be considered "joy"? It was not because it was easy since He "endured the cross" and "endured such hostility from sinners against Himself" (Heb. 12:3). Isaiah speaks in graphic terms of His pain and suffering (Isaiah 53). Our present verse tells us that He was "despising the shame." These do not sound like terms of joy.

We must remember that joy is not dependent on external circumstances. Jesus was not "happy" about the cross, yet He could view it with joy. Jesus found delight in doing the Father's will (John 4:34; Heb. 10:9). The cross was the Father's will and Jesus' purpose for coming (John 12:27). It was "joy" therefore to complete the Father's will. In addition, Jesus was glorified because of His sacrifice (John 12:23–24; Phil. 2:8–11). His glorification (John 17:1–5) was certainly reason for joy. The way of the cross led to glory.

Yet another benefit, and one which causes us to rejoice as well, is that the cross meant the payment for our sins and the offer of salvation. It was love that nailed Jesus to the cross (John 3:16). Jesus could view the cross with joy because He loved us and knew that His suffering there would enable us to have forgiveness for our sins and an eternal home with Him in Heaven. Jesus' joy was related to doing the Father's will. His glorification and our justification are benefits. Now those are terms of joy!

As Jesus found joy in doing the Father's will, so can we. Doing God's will does not always mean suffering, but even when it does, we can be joyful. Paul, in prison and expecting execution because of his preaching and testimony for the Lord, wrote to the Philippians: "Yes, and I am being poured out as a drink offering on the sacrifice and service of your faith, I am glad and rejoice with you all" (Phil. 2:17).

Every believer has the capacity for joy, even in adversity. Those who are missing it may have been looking in the wrong place. A man asked his friend one day why he always seemed to be so joyful. The friend answered that it was because of his good looks. When the first man looked surprised (and doubtful), the friend explained: "First, I'm looking unto Jesus, the author and finisher of our faith . . . and second, I'm looking for that blessed hope, and the glorious appearing of the great God and our Savior Jesus Christ."

In times of adversity, joy is hard won. Joni Eareckson Tada recorded the following story in *Decision* Magazine. "Honesty is always the best policy, but especially when you're surrounded by a crowd of women in a restroom during a break at a Christian women's conference. One woman, putting on lipstick, said, 'Oh, Joni, you always look so together, so happy in your wheelchair. I wish I had your joy!' Several women around her nodded. 'How *do* you do it?' she asked as she capped her lipstick.

"I *don't* do it," I said. "In fact, may I tell you honestly how I woke up this morning? This is an average day: After my husband, Ken, leaves for work at 6:00 A.M., I'm alone until I hear the front door open at 7:00 A.M. That's when a friend arrives to get me up. While I listen to her make coffee, I pray, 'Oh, Lord, my friend will soon give me a bath, get me dressed, sit me up in my chair, brush my hair and teeth, and send me out the door. I don't have the strength to face this routine one more time. I have no resources. I don't have a smile to take into the day. But You do. May I have Yours? God, I need you desperately.'"

"So, what happens when your friend comes through the bedroom door?" one of them asked.

"I turn my head toward her and give her a smile sent straight from heaven. It's not mine. It's God's. And so," I said gesturing to my paralyzed legs, "whatever joy you see today was hard won this morning."

WE NEED TO ANTICIPATE GOD'S WORKING

To the Jews in captivity who wondered if God really knew their plight, if He was powerful enough to do something, and if He could and would still work, God answered:

> "To whom then will you liken Me, or to whom shall I be equal?" says the Holy One. Lift up your eyes on high, And see who has created these things, Who brings out their host by number, He calls them all by name, by the greatness of His might and the strength of His power, not one is missing.
>
> Why do you say, O Jacob, and speak, O Israel: "My way is hidden from the Lord, and my just claim is passed over by God?"
>
> Have you not known? Have you not heard? The everlasting God, the Lord, The Creator of the ends of the earth, neither faints nor is weary. There is no searching of His understanding.
>
> (Isaiah 40:25–28)

The message is clear: God is God; there is no one like Him; He even calls each star by its name (we can't even count or see them all!), He is eternal in His being, knowledge and power, He has created all things and upholds all things, He never gets tired, He is God. God's answer to the questioning captives was for them to anticipate His working. The same God who answered them answers us in our times of adversity. We need to anticipate God's working.

As we shall see in this chapter, God works in unseen ways; He works in unknown ways; His working is perfect; His working is continuous, and His working is promised.

Just because we do not see something does not mean it is not there. None of us can actually see electricity moving, since it travels at the speed of light, but we would not doubt its presence or moving or power when we flip a switch and a light turns on. There are light rays beyond the grasp of our eyes and there are sound waves beyond the capacity of our ears, yet we would not doubt their existence. Likewise, just because we do not physically see God's hand at work does not mean it is not there.

The King of Syria feared the prophet Elisha and wanted to elimi-nate him so that he might attack Israel. We read the following amazing account:

> Therefore he sent horses and chariots and a great army there, and they came by night and surrounded the city. And when the servant of the man of God arose early and went out, there was an army, surround-ing the city with horses and chariots. And his servant said to him, "Alas, my master! What shall we do?" So he answered, "Do not fear, for those who are with us are more than those who are with them." And Elisha prayed, and said, "Lord I pray, open his eyes that he may see." Then the Lord opened the eyes of the young man, and he saw. And behold, the mountain was full of horses and chariots of fire all around Elisha.
>
> (2 Kings 6:14–17)

We may be surrounded by chariots of fire and not even realize it. We see only the tip of the iceberg of what God is doing. What we need is not more vision to see, but more faith to trust. God works in unseen ways. At times He is gracious to let us see what He is doing or how He is working, but He is not obligated to show us. Often it is more like the electricity; we see the results but not the flow of energy.

Stan was a hard case. He scoffed when I told him about Jesus. He was a tough guy and didn't need "the crutch of religion," as he put it. I kept working and praying and trying. I finally gave up. If anything, Stan seemed to be increasing in his vices and decreasing in his patience with me. I gave up—but God didn't. Stan eventually came to know the Lord. He confessed to me that from the very first time we had talked, he was convicted to the bone. I had no way of knowing that. I couldn't see it, but God was working on the inside. God continued to hammer away at that stony heart. As conviction increased, Stan made an increased effort to delve into his sins and get rid of God. I gave up because I couldn't see. God kept working and Stan became one of His own.

There may be people or circumstances that seem like impossible cases to you. Perhaps you have worked and prayed and tried to no avail. It seems hopeless. In such cases we need to realize that God can work in ways unseen and unperceived by us. What we see on the outside may not tell the whole story.

God not only works in unseen ways, He works in unknown ways. They may be unknown because they are unseen. Another possibility is that God's ways are just beyond our understanding. Returning to a passage we have examined elsewhere, we see clearly the difference that lies between our understanding and God's. Isaiah wrote:

> "For My thoughts are not your thoughts. Nor are your ways My ways," says the Lord. "For as the heavens are higher than the earth, so are My ways higher than your ways, and My thoughts than your thoughts."
>
> (Isaiah 55:8–9)

Though I am not very good at it, I enjoy playing chess. I remember (with some humiliation) the first chess tournament I played in. God allowed me to play in the first round against the fellow who eventually won first place for the tournament. I knew some basic moves, but at first this poor fellow didn't seem to me to know what he was doing. I decided to go for the quick kill and not make him suffer long. I advanced my queen to a good point of attack. In three moves I not only lost my queen, but was put in checkmate. This guy was working in ways unknown to me, in fact, in ways which at that time did not make good sense to me.

God works in ways which are unknown to us. We may not realize why He is doing what He is doing or how He is doing it, but our responsibility is not to figure God out, but to trust Him and anticipate His working. No one can checkmate our King!

We should anticipate God's working since "As for God, His way is perfect . . ." (Psalm 18:30). We cannot anticipate God working in exactly the way *we* want Him to work. We can, however, be confident that what He does will not only be right, but perfect.

Moses sang one last song to Israel before God took him home. That song is recorded in Deuteronomy 32. One of the first items Moses sang about was the perfection of God's ways and works.

> For I proclaim the name of the Lord: Ascribe greatness to our God.
> He is the Rock, His work is perfect; For all His ways are justice, a God
> of truth and without injustice; Righteous and upright is He.
>
> (Deut. 32:3–4)

Moses, who had been in the valley as well as the mountaintop, could sum up all that God had done with "His work is perfect." Not a single flaw was to be found. Moses' life was far from being an easy one, yet he was able to proclaim at the end of it "for all His ways are justice."

God does not make mistakes. Second guessing Him as to timing, purpose, operation, etc., is not only futile, but harmful. Anticipating not only that He will work, but also that what He does will be perfect is a great source of comfort and encouragement.

It may be helpful to go through the following questions in your own mind and heart to see how you stand.

Do I believe God *can* work?

Do I believe God *will* work all things according to His will?

Do I believe that *whatever* God does will be perfect?

If you answer "no" to any of the above, you need to work on that area more. If you answer "yes" to all the above, you have the foundation for peace in your heart. When you sense that peace slipping, go back and ask those three questions again to determine what happened. God will not change, "He is the Rock, His work is perfect."

God's working is not only perfect, it is continuous. He not only spoke the light into being, he provides continual light. Since the beginning, there has never been a day without the sun or night without the moon and stars. God not only created the heaven and the earth and all that is in them, He holds it all together by His own power (Col. 1:16–17; Heb. 1:2–3, 11:3). God does not abandon His works; He upholds them by the power of His hand.

What may be said of creation is certainly to be applied to the new creation, namely believers. God's working is continuous. The Lord teaches us this principle through Paul when he writes: "Being confident of this very thing, that He who has begun a good work in you will complete it until the day of Jesus Christ" (Phil 1:6).

This is not an idea we need to wonder about or question. Indeed, we can be "confident of this very thing" with Paul. The Lord does not give up on His own. He will never leave us or forsake us. We can be completely confident that He will continue to work in our lives. We, therefore, should certainly anticipate His working.

Who began the good work in the lives of the Philippians? It was not Paul. It was not some other Apostle or missionary. It was God. The One who began the good work in our own lives was God. It helps to recapture that thought. Man will let us down. Even the one who first introduced us to the Lord may let us down tomorrow. But our confidence is not in them, it is in God. He began the work and He will continue it.

How long will He continue to work in our lives? Paul answers: "until the day of Jesus Christ." As the saying goes: "it ain't over till it's over." We need to keep growing in the Lord and closer to the Lord. When we look just like Christ, then we have reached the goal (Phil. 3:12–214; Eph. 4:12–13). That moment will not arrive for any of us "until the day of Jesus Christ." Until then, "it is God who works in you both to will and to do of His good pleasure" (Phil. 2:13).

We can and should anticipate God's working. He works at times and in unseen and unknown ways. His working is both perfect and continuous. Added to this are the promises of God. We need to claim His promises. We need to lay hold of them by faith. We need to anticipate His working because He has promised to do so.

It will help us to consider several categories of God's promises. Just as it is important to realize what God has promised, it is important for us to understand what He has *not* promised. God never promised that we would not experience trials, tribulations, adversity, illness, death, persecution, financial loss, or disappointment in life. In fact, the Lord indicated that we could *expect* such difficulties (John 16:33; Rom. 8:36; etc.). That doesn't sound very comforting, does it? Our hope, however, is not in being shielded from adversity, but rather having victory *in* adversity. That is why Paul wrote: "Yet *in* all these things we are more than conquerors through Him who loved us" (Rom. 8:37) and "Blessed be the God and Father of our Lord Jesus Christ . . . who comforts us *in* all our tribulation . . ." (2 Cor. 1:4). We are comforted, encouraged, sustained, and victorious *in* adversity because God has promised His presence, His provision, and His power. A verse which expresses all three areas of promise is Isaiah 41:10, which reads: "Fear not, for I am with you; be not dismayed, for I am your God. I will strengthen you, yes, I will help you, I will uphold you with my righteous right hand."

We don't want to walk through the valley or through the dark alone. The promise of God is that we will not (Ps. 23:4). God says that the *reason* we are not to fear adversity or even death is because of His continual presence (Josh. 1:9; Isa. 41:10, 43:2–5; Ps. 9:9–10, 139:7–12; John 10:28; Acts 18:9–10; Rom. 8:38–39). Over and over again God reminds us that He is always with us.

I remember as a child being afraid to go to an empty house down the block. It had been abandoned for some time and fostered many wild imaginings. When I was with my buddies, however, I was much bolder. Their presence made a big difference. Even today as a pastor, as I go to other "strange" houses on visitation, I sense that I am less anxious if I have someone with me.

God has not intended that we move through life's experiences alone. Though all the world forsake us, He is always there. We do not need to fear. The reason for our boldness is not arrogance, but trust in God's presence. After all, safety is not the absence of danger but the presence of God!

In our time of need we can also trust in the promise of God's provision. Paul wrote to the believers at Philippi: "And my God shall supply all your need according to His riches in glory by Christ Jesus" (Phil. 4:19). The idea of God's provision and our need to trust in that provision is given most extensively by Jesus in His Sermon on the Mount. In one portion, He says:

> Therefore I say to you, do not worry about your life, what you will eat or what you will drink: nor about your body, what you will put on. Is not life more than food and the body more than clothing? Look at the birds of the air, for they neither sow nor reap nor gather into barns: yet your heavenly Father feeds them. Are you not of more value than they? Which of you by worrying can add one cubit to his stature? So why do you worry about clothing? Consider the lilies of the field, how they grow; they neither toil nor spin; and yet I say to you that even Solomon in all his glory was not arrayed like one of these. Now if God so clothed the grass of the field, which today is, and tomorrow is thrown into the oven, will He not much more clothe you, O you of little faith? Therefore do not worry, saying, "What shall we eat? or What shall we drink? or What shall we wear?" For after all these things the Gentiles seek. For your heavenly Father knows that you need all these things. But seek first the kingdom of God and His righteousness, and all these things shall be added to you. Therefore do not worry about tomorrow, for tomorrow will worry about its own things. Sufficient for the day is its own trouble.
>
> (Matt. 6:25–34)

The Lord knows how to take care of His own. He is more aware of our needs than we are, and He is infinitely more capable of meeting them. On a number of occasions when we as a family have had our backs against the wall and could see no way out, my wife, Sherrie, has exclaimed (almost incredulously to the rest of us)! "Isn't this exciting? Now we will see what God can do!" She has always been right, not because she is a prophetess or the daughter of one, but because she firmly believes that God is faithful and He has promised His provision for our needs.

God has not only promised to be with us and to provide for us, He has promised us *His* power. We have already experienced the dismal strength that lies within ourselves. What we need everyday, and especially in times of adversity, is God's strength.

In the verse we began with (Isa. 41:10), God promised: ". . . . I will strengthen you, yes I will help you, I will uphold you with My righteous right hand." Other verses which echo this promise are Philippians 4:13: "I can do all things through Christ who strengthens me"; Ephesians 6:10: "Finally, my brethren, be strong in the Lord and in the power of His might"; Colossians 1:11: "Strengthened with all might according to His glorious power, for all patience and longsuffering with joy." Our strength must come from the Lord for as He said ". . . without me you can do nothing" (John 15:5) and ". . . with God all things are possible" (Matt. 19:26).

Since God has promised His presence, His provision, and His power, we are filled with hope and live in anticipation of His working. Now we will see what God can do!

> There is an eye that never sleeps
> Beneath the wing of night;
> There is an ear that never shuts
> When sink the beams of light
>
> There is an arm that never tires
> When human strength gives way;
> There is a love that never fails
> When earthly loves decay.
>
> That eye is fixed on seraph throngs;
> That ear is filled with angel's songs;
> That arm upholds the worlds on high;
> That love is thron'd beyond the sky.

Heber

WE NEED TO DO WHAT WE CAN

There is an Arab fable which tells of a man who, while walking through the forest, saw a fox that had lost its legs. He wondered how it survived. Then he saw a tiger come in with game in its mouth. The tiger had its fill and left the rest of the meat for the fox. The next day God fed the fox by means of the same tiger. The man began to wonder at God's great goodness and said to himself, "I, too, shall just rest in a corner with full trust in the Lord and He will provide me with all I need." He did this for many days, but nothing happened, and the poor fellow was almost at death's door when he heard a Voice say, "O you are in the path of error, open your eyes to the truth! Follow the example of the tiger and stop imitating the disabled fox."

Trusting God does not release us from the responsibility of doing what we can. Both are needed. As Jesus told the Pharisees, ". . . These you ought to have done, without leaving the others undone" (Matt. 23:23). It is not a matter of either/or, but both. God expects us to do the possible, and to trust Him for the impossible.

Defining those areas and situations which are "possible" for us to do something about is a complicated and subjective task. Some cases are easy to determine. Remember the problem of the mousetrap on the unsuspecting finger? The solution is straightforward: remove it as soon as possible. I do not know of anyone who would have trouble coming to that conclusion.

Most of the situations we face are not so easily handled. On a higher level of difficulty, let's say a man, John, has lost his job. What should he do? Certainly, he should seek other employment. There is a difference between this situation and the mousetrap though. If John had the mousetrap on his finger, we would not think it strange for him to remove it without taking time to pray over the matter. Seeking other employment, however, should be done in praying for God's guidance and trusting for His provision and direction. Applications should be covered in prayer.

The more removed our control of the situation is, the more complex and difficult our decisions become. At the extreme, we may feel totally frustrated in trying to make a decision or doing anything. Someone suffering from a life-threatening illness, who has the possibility before them of undergoing a very risky (and expensive) operation which would be followed up with extensive treatments known to cause severe side effects, has a very difficult decision to make. *They* can do nothing. Their one contribution is to decide, and even that is based on someone else's observations. At this level, it becomes obvious and acute that prayer and trust must play a major role. The patient *can* pray; the patient *can* trust.

We must learn to do what we can. Sometimes it will be very much and other times it will be very little. Each person is different and each situation presents a different set of circumstances, challenges, obstacles, relationships, possibilities, concerns, personalities, and problems. One's education, for instance, has nothing to do with removing a mousetrap or cancer, but has much to do with finding employment.

When Jesus said "Lazarus, come forth!" (John 11:43), He demonstrated the same divine power which also spoke all creation into existence. That He even spoke out loud was only for our benefit, not because it was necessary for the miracle (John 11:41–42). Imagine the astonishment of the onlookers as "he who had died came out" (John 11:44). Jesus had done what they could not do. Jesus had done the impossible.

Both before and after this striking miracle, Jesus gave a command for those standing around the scene to get involved, to do what they could. First, He instructed them to "take away the stone" (John 11:39). After the raising of Lazarus, since Lazarus was "bound hand and foot with graveclothes, and his face was wrapped with a cloth, Jesus said to them, 'Loose him, and let him go'" (John 11:44). Now, He who could raise the dead, could easily have moved the stone and removed the graveclothes. Why didn't He? He was teaching them more than one lesson that glorious day, and one of those lessons was: you do the possible, and trust Me for the impossible.

When the four friends brought their lame companion to Jesus, they had a rough time (Mark 2:2–12). Jesus was not taken by surprise at these events. He could have gone out to them or commanded that the crowd make way for them. But He didn't. He allowed them to do what they could. He gave them opportunity to display their faith, which He noted (Mark 2:5). He allowed a story to unroll which would be an inspiration to other believers throughout the ages. The four men may have wondered why they had to go through so much; Jesus knew why. They would do the possible; He would do the impossible. Is God teaching you the same lesson?

I was recently visiting with a family in our church when their teen-age son came in all excited. He had been incubating some chicken eggs and one of them now had a small hole in it. His father explained why patience was necessary. To help the baby chick get out would do more damage than good. The chick needed the struggle and the stretching experience in order to rightly develop its wings. To "help" would be to hinder what God had built in the system to strengthen the chick for life in the real world. It was not only possible for the chick to eventually get out of that tight space, but the very process of exiting was designed for its good.

Our heavenly Father wants us to do what we can do. It is not because He does not care about our struggle. It is not because He could not help us out of a tight spot. God knows that our needs go beyond our immediate deliverance. He knows that we need stretching experiences as an aid to our development. He knows that the process of struggling can strengthen our character. We have an advantage over the chicken. It is not aware of the help it is getting from the heat of the incubator. It is not aware of the presence of a much interested observer. We, however, can trust that our Lord is watching over the whole process and that He will not allow us to drown. As He promised Israel: "When you pass through the waters, I will be with you; and through the rivers, they shall not overflow you. When you walk through the fire, you shall not be burned, nor shall the flame scorch you? (Isaiah 43:2).

Prayer and trust are essential. Sometimes, perhaps most times, the Lord wants us to respond in *active* faith. If you have lost a job, apply for another one. If your wife has left you, seek to be reconciled. If you are ill, seek medical attention. Whatever your situation, do what you can. Move forward in faith, relying on God's strength to do what you can, what He wants you to do, praying as you go for direction and discernment, trusting that as you do the possible, God will do the impossible.

CONCLUSION / SUMMARY

Sometimes, as the saying goes, it is hard to see the forest for the trees. We have been looking at different appropriate responses a believer should make in times of adversity. The problem is, by examining each response closely and individually, we tend to lose the overall picture. It reminds me of the story of the blind men who were given the task of describing an elephant. One man examined the tail and reported that an elephant is like a rope. Another man felt the sides and concluded that an elephant is like a wall. Another man took hold of a leg and determined that an elephant resembles a tree. The fourth man inspected the trunk and described an elephant as a large water hose.

It would be well for us to briefly look at each piece of the puzzle and thus try to put together a coherent picture which is both more accurate and more valuable than its individual parts. Except for the first point, the responses are not arranged in any order of priority.

1. We need to view Christ as the center of our lives to the point that everything else, even our health and life, becomes of secondary importance. This is not to say that our adversity does not hurt or has no importance. It is to say that Christ, and not ourselves or our problems, must be center. As my friend, Dr. Donald

155

Whitney, recently explained during a message at my church, "Christ is not simply first on an unending list of priorities in our lives; He is the *center of everything* in our lives." Without this step, the rest will be difficult, if not impossible.

2. We need to recognize God at work in our lives in the bad times as well as the good times. Just because things have gone wrong does not mean God is not there or that He is not interested and active in our lives. In fact, He may be using the very adversity we are under to mold our character and to make us more Christ-like.

3. We need to look for the good in everything. This is not to say that everything is good, but that God can work in all things together for good. What is He seeking to accomplish in my life through this adversity? Also, instead of concentrating on the negatives, we need to stop and count our blessings.

4. We need to examine our lives for unconfessed sins since adversity may relate to discipline. If there are none apparent, ask God to search your heart and convict you. If there is not improvement, then the adversity is not related to sin and/or God has a further purpose in allowing it to linger. At any rate, a good spiritual checkup is never out of order!

5. We need to pray. Prayer is vital; it is not an option. We need to pray for our needs, requests, strength, direction, healing, and most important, God's will. We also need to earnestly pray for one another.

6. We need to trust. Trusting God means you believe that He will be faithful to His Word. Trust is in direct proportion to peace: the more trust we have, the more peace we have. Trusting God for the outcome is more important than knowing.

7. We need to be content in whatever situation we are in. Jesus was able to be content in the boat during the storm because He knew His life and destiny were in the Father's hands. God is still on His throne. Being content does not mean we do not seek to change an adverse situation when we can. For example, a sick person should see a doctor and take medicine, if needed.

8. We need to be patient. Lack of patience means that our timetable does not correspond with God's. In that case, who has the right

timing? It is by being still that we can best see the hand of God. Tribulation teaches patience—learn the lesson early!

9. We need to be steadfast. The only way to stand fast in the storm is to have the right foundation, and to cling to the Cross. A lack of steadfastness only leads to more woes.

10. We need to be joyful. It is possible to be joyful (not happy) in the midst of tribulation. We can be joyful that God does not leave us or give up on us, we can be joyful that we were counted worthy to suffer for His name, we can be joyful that we have an eternal life awaiting us that knows no pain or sorrow, we can be joyful that no external circumstances can touch the internal peace of resting in God.

11. We need to anticipate God's working. He works in unseen and unknown ways at times. His working is perfect, continuous, and promised. He promises His presence, His power, and His provision.

12. We need to do what we can. By prayer and trust we do what is possible for us to do (by God's grace and enablement) and we trust what is impossible to our Lord. We are responsible for our part, and we can be certain that God will take care of His.

Notes

[1]Gary Inrig, *A Call to Excellence* (Wheaton, IL: Scripture Press, 1985), p. 152.

[2]Stanley C. Baldwin, *Bruised But Not Broken* (Portland, OR: Multnomah, 1985), pp. 107–9.

[3]C. E. B. Cranfield, *Romans, A Shorter Commentary* (Grand Rapids, MI: Eerdmans, 1985), p. 204.

[4]Ibid.

[5]S. D. Gordon, *Quiet Talks on Prayer* (New York: Pyramid, 1967), p. 27.

[6]Gerhard Kittle and Gerhard Friedrich, *Theological Dictionary of the New Testament,* translated by Geoffrey W. Bromiley (Grand Rapids, MI: Eerdmans, 1985), p. 144.

[7]Jack Taylor, *Prayer: Life's Limitless Reach* (Nashville, TN: Broadman, 1977), p. 140.

[8]Ibid., p. 27.

[9]David McCasland, "One to Grow On" in *Power For Living* (Glen Ellyn, IL: Scripture Press, Oct. 9, 1988), p. 8.

[10]Gary R. Collins, *Christian Counseling: A Comprehensive Guide* (Waco, TX: Word, 1980), p. 102.

[11]AFA Journal, P.O. Drawer 2440, Tupelo, MS 38803. Executive Editor: Donald Wildmon. AFA is a Christian organization promoting the biblical ethic of decency in American society with primary emphasis on TV and other media.

PART THREE:

Practical Questions Related to Adversity in the Life of a Believer

There are a number of practical questions which naturally arise when a believer faces adversity. Many of these questions are not directly related to any biblical mandate or principle. For instance, if a person's house is destroyed by a tornado, a practical question might be whether to rebuild in the city or in the country. A number of options, benefits, and liabilities would need to be considered, but we would look in vain to find a biblical direction. That is *not* to say that God does not have a will in such matters. The person should pray and seek the Lord's leading in the decision.

Other questions are related to a biblical teaching or principle. In this section we will examine twelve such questions. These are not by any means the only questions which have biblical answers. They are questions which I, as a pastor, have frequently been asked. These twelve questions are:

1. How far will God allow us to go in situations involving suffering or hardship?
2. Will a Christian experience less adversity than a non-Christian?
3. Should we pray for, or expect, or demand healing for someone who is seriously ill?
4. If "the end of our lives is in God's hands," why seek help?
5. Are "faith healers" for real?
6. Will modern science and medicine ever wipe out sickness?
7. How can I be a testimony to others when I don't feel well?
8. What about life support systems and euthanasia?
9. How should I respond to the AIDS problem?
10. What if I am being persecuted—what should I do?
11. Should I take another believer to court?
12. Death—the last enemy; the final question.

It is not likely that all of these questions would be in the mind of one given individual at the same time. It is likely, though, that each of us will either directly experience most of these questions at some time or minister to those who do. They warrant careful and biblical consideration. God has an answer; let's seek to discover it.

How Far Will God Allow Us to Go in Situations Involving Hardship or Suffering?

Will God allow us to die? Do you have a life insurance policy? If you do, you know the answer to that question. Ever since the sin of Adam and Eve, death has reigned. "Therefore, just as through one man sin entered the world, and death through sin, and thus death spread to all men, because all sinned" (Romans 5:12). The writer of Hebrews reminds us that ". . . it is appointed for men to die once, but after this the judgment" (Heb. 9:27). The phrase "to die once" eliminates the false concept of reincarnation. It also very simply and bleakly informs us of our common destiny—the grave.

Death is not an option, but whether it is viewed as a friend or foe depends on our relationship with the Lord. This topic will be more thoroughly covered in the last chapter. For now, we will turn our attention to less drastic, but potentially more difficult situations.

Many of us have gone through trials which seemed so dark and hard and prolonged that we began to wonder if there would ever be any light, any easing up, and hopefully ending of the trial. To take one more step, to endure one more day, was more weight than we could bear. Perhaps at such a time a friend reminded us, or we read on our own, the promise of 1 Corinthians 10:13. To paraphrase (which is usually the case when this verse is used): God will not allow more to come into our lives than He knows we will be able to take. The problem is, that is not what the verse says. The fact is, God *will* allow us to go through more than we can take *in our own strength*. Why? Because we need to lean on Him and trust in Him and not ourselves. If God never allowed us to go through trials bigger than we are and beyond our own capacity to bear, we would never learn to really trust Him.

What, then, is the promise of 1 Corinthians 10:13? It is related directly to temptations, not to trials. (For the distinction between the two, see the introduction to Part Two.) This is seen both in the wording of the verse itself and in the immediate context.

The verse says: "No temptation has overtaken you except such as is common to man; but God is faithful, who will not allow you to be tempted beyond what you are able, but with the temptation will also make the way of escape, that you may be able to bear it." Notice that the word "trial" never appears, but that "temptation" appears twice and "tempted" appears once. The promise is not that we would not go through trials too difficult for us, but that we would not be subjected to temptations so great that we would *have* to give in and have no choice but to sin.

Paul gives five reasons why we will not undergo overwhelming temptations. The first reason is that all temptations are "such as is common to man." There is no such thing as a "supernatural" temptation.

The second reason is that "God is faithful." Things change, moods change, people change, circumstances change, needs change, times change, and our vulnerability changes; *but* the Rock that does not change is our Lord. He is always faithful. If we are founded and steadfast on Him, there is no temptation which in itself will *force* us off that foundation.

The third reason why we will not undergo overwhelming temptations is that God sets the limits. As Paul expressed it, "[He] will not allow you to be tempted beyond what you are able." A great example is the life of Job. "What you are able" does not mean just on your own. You, as a believer, have resources. God intends for you to use them (spiritual armor, the Holy Spirit, Christian friends, etc.).

The fourth reason is that there is an option to giving in to temptation—escape! God "will also make the way of escape." Escape from
what? Sin.

The fifth reason is that God will enable you to bear it. The word
"bear" means to "endure." The idea is not that we would necessarily go
around every temptation, but that in God's strength we can go *through*
any temptation that He allows to come our way.

The context of the twelve verses preceding the verse in question very
definitely relates to the temptation of the Jews in the wilderness. Paul's
point is to learn from their mistakes and not give in to temptation like
they did (see especially v. 6). The very next verse after 1 Cor. 10:13 says
"Therefore, my beloved, flee from idolatry." Again, it is speaking not
of trials, but of temptation.

It is good for us that this promise does relate to temptations rather
than trials. Trials are not pleasant, but they are useful in causing us to
cling to the Cross. Temptations may often be pleasant for a moment,
but they can be destructive to our spiritual well-being. Praise God that
we will not be overwhelmed by temptation to the point that we must
give in!

Our hope is not based on any promise that we will not suffer affliction, nor that our tribulations would only be as great as we ourselves
could bear. The testimony of Scripture is rather that nothing shall
separate us from Christ or His love, and in that great love we are more
than victorious. Paul put it this way:

> Who shall separate us from the love of Christ? Shall tribulation, or
> distress, or persecution, or famine, or nakedness, or peril, or sword?
> As it is written: "For Your sake we are killed all day long; we are ac-
> counted as sheep for the slaughter." Yet in all these things we are more
> than conquerors through Him who loved us. For I am persuaded that
> neither death nor life, nor angels, nor principalities, nor powers, nor
> things to come, nor height, nor depth, nor any other created thing,
> shall be able to separate us from the love of God which is in Christ
> Jesus our Lord.
>
> (Romans 8:35–39)

Lest we paint too bleak a picture, we must gain a proper perspective. In the midst of trials it is hard to see. We need to gain a foothold up and rise above the fray for a minute. What we find is that, although we are not promised a life without adversity, illness, loss, or trials, we know that our God will work out that which is right and best and needful in our lives.

God is not trying to see how miserable He can make our lives. Remember that many, if not most, of our woes are self-inflicted! God is our heavenly Father who will not give a stone to His child who asks for bread (Matt. 7:9–11), Who knows our needs (Matt. 6:31) and Who meets those needs (Phil. 4:19). He does not enjoy seeing His children suffer anymore than you would delight in your child's suffering. He is gracious beyond measure. His ways and works are perfect. He knows all things. His love never fails. He rules over all. Nothing will come into your life that He does not know about for it must first pass through His hands.

I remember when our dog, Ginger, had her first litter of puppies. She watched over them carefully. She would let me or my wife take one of them, but she watched us very closely. A stranger was met with a low growl if they even approached a puppy. The slightest cry caught Ginger's immediate attention. God watches over us infinitely more carefully than Ginger watched over her puppies. He not only hears our slightest cry, He knows before we cry, and He knows why we cry, and He understands the depth of our cry. As the psalmist David wrote of God: "You number my wanderings; put my tears into Your bottle; are they not in Your book?" (Ps. 56:8).

How far will God allow us to go in situations involving suffering or hardship? That is impossible to say. Every situation and person is different. That which remains constant is God. Our hope, therefore, is not that we will not endure hardships beyond our own capability to handle them, but that when we do, we know that God is faithful and our trust is in Him. Psalm 56:11 says, "In God I have put my trust. I will not be afraid."

WILL A CHRISTIAN EXPERIENCE LESS ADVERSITY THAN AN UNBELIEVER?

A local factory was forced by economic considerations to lay off many of its employees for an indefinite period of time. When the axe fell, it came down on believers and unbelievers alike. All who had fewer than five years on the job, regardless of their relationship with God, were let go.

Joe came to my office complaining and wondering why God had allowed him, His child, to lose his much-needed job.

Joe had a hard time accepting the principle which Solomon presented nearly three thousand years ago:

> Everything occurs alike to all: One event happens to the righteous and the wicked; To the good, the clean, and to the unclean; To him who sacrifices and to him who does not sacrifice. As is the good, so is the sinner; and he who takes an oath as he who fears an oath."
>
> (Eccl. 9:2)

God does not guarantee immunity to hardship just because we belong to Him. To take Joe's logic (that a believer should be protected by his heavenly Father from earthly problems) to its extreme, we would end up with a society in which no believer was ever ill, ever had an accident, ever lost a job, ever died, ever needed to trust, ever needed to obey or ever knew the sustaining grace of God.

So how about this question—*will* a Christian experience less adversity than an unbeliever?

The answer to the above question will depend to some degree on the individual Christian's situation. A believer in China, for example, may face great persecution. His life may be more miserable (from a human and physical standpoint) than his unbelieving counterpart. In general, however, I would have to say yes—a Christian will probably experience less adversity than an unbeliever.

There are a number of experiences, both good and bad, that believers share with unbelievers. We know that God ". . . makes His sun rise on the evil and on the good, and sends rain on the just and on the unjust" (Matt. 5:45). We know also that we *all* suffer from the consequence of living in a sin-filled world (tornadoes, plagues, drought, etc.—see chapter one). So far, the scale is even between believers and unbelievers. We all buy cold medicine. But as we consider some other areas, the scale tends to dip in our favor, except for cases of severe persecution. The practical result of sin should be a concern more for an unbeliever than a believer. That is not to say that believers do not sin. Neither does that mean that believers should not be concerned over the practical results of sin in their lives. We are not sinless, but we should sin less and less as we grow in grace and in the knowledge of Jesus Christ our Lord. Unbelievers have much more cause for concern because of their sinful life-style and practices. God at least allows, if not causes, sinners to suffer the consequences of their evil deeds. Paul spoke very pointedly to this issue when he wrote:

> Do not be deceived, God is not mocked; for whatever a man sows, that he will also reap. For he who sows to his flesh will of the flesh reap corruption, but he who sows to the Spirit will of the Spirit reap everlasting life. And let us not grow weary while doing good, for in due season we shall reap if we do not lose heart.
>
> (Galatians 6:7–9)

We reap the good things we sow and the principle holds true as well for the bad things we sow. An unbeliever is in the confirmed pattern of sowing to the flesh. Sometimes the result is an immediate catastrophe. Often the result is a storing up of woes until they come crashing down in some adversity (Romans 2:5).

God does not let sin just kind of slide by. There is a day of reckoning.

> Then I saw a great white throne and Him who sat on it, from whose face the earth and the heaven fled away. And there was found no place for them. And I saw the dead, small and great, standing before God, and books were opened. And another book was opened, which is the Book of Life. And the dead were judged according to their works, by the things which were written in the books. The sea gave up the dead who were in it, and Death and Hades delivered up the dead who were in them. And they were judged, each one according to his works. Then Death and Hades were cast into the lake of fire. This is the second death. And anyone not found written in the Book of Life was cast into the lake of fire.
>
> (Revelation 20:11–15)

The *reason* these people will be brought before the great white throne is that they did not accept God's sacrifice for their sins; therefore, their names were "not found written in the Book of Life . . ." They will face eternal adversity, to put it mildly! Who will have less adversity in the long run? It should be obvious that a believer will end up with much less adversity. Even in the case of a persecuted believer, ten thousand years from now the unbeliever will have long since passed him in the amount of adversity.

Not only is there a payment for sin at the end of life, but there is a payment of a different sort throughout life. Consider these words from Paul:

> For the wrath of God is revealed from heaven against all ungodliness and unrighteousness of men, who suppress the truth in unrighteousness, because what may be known of God is manifest in them, for God has shown it to them. For since the creation of the world His invisible attributes are clearly seen, being understood by the things that are made, even His eternal power and Godhead, so that they are without excuse, because, although they knew God, they did not glorify Him

as God, nor were thankful, but became futile in their thoughts, and their foolish hearts were darkened. Professing to be wise, they became fools, and changed the glory of the incorruptible God into an image made like corruptible man—and birds and four-footed beasts and creeping things. Therefore God also gave them up to uncleanness, in the lusts of their hearts, to dishonor their bodies among themselves, who exchanged the truth of God for the lie, and worshiped and served the creature rather than the Creator, who is blessed forever. Amen. For this reason God gave them up to vile passions. For even their women exchanged the natural use for what is against nature. Likewise also the men, leaving the natural use of the woman, burned in their lust for one another, men with men committing what is shameful, and receiving in themselves the penalty of their error which was due.

(Romans 1:18–27)

This last verse, Romans 1:27, could be especially appropriate for our AIDS epidemic. Many who have indulged in sinful homosexual practices have reaped the penalty of AIDS. It is almost alarming to read those last words: "which was due." The AIDS problem and how to respond will be considered in a later chapter.

Problems related to the excessive consumption of alcoholic beverages are reserved for unbelievers. That is not to say that no believer would drink an alcoholic beverage, but that if he does, he is shunning the joy and peace that could be his and is claiming in their place the woes of a drinker. If you want to avoid unnecessary adversity, stay away from sinful practices.

Let's ask the wisest man in the world if drinking alcoholic beverages leads to problems.

Who has woe? Who has sorrow? Who has contentions? Who has complaints? Who has wounds without cause? Who has redness of eyes? Those who linger long at the wine, those who go in search of mixed wine. Do not look on the wine when it is red, when it sparkles in the cup, when it swirls around smoothly; at the last it bites like a serpent, and stings like a viper. Your eyes will see strange things, and your heart will utter perverse things. Yes, you will be like one who lies down in the midst of the sea, or like one who lies at the top of the mast, saying: "They have struck me, but I was not hurt; They have

beaten me, but I did not feel it. When shall I awake, that I may seek
another drink?"

(Proverbs 23:29–35)

The problems related to alcohol go beyond just the physical problems attached to the drinker, although that in itself should be deterrent enough. There are also the consequent problems, such as broken homes, lost jobs, and ruined relationships. Driving while under the influence of alcohol can result in a lost license or even lost lives.

There are numerous such examples of how lifestyle and sinful practices lead to more potential adversity in the life of an unbeliever than in the life of a believer. Besides the obvious physical and outward show of problems, there is also the emotional and psychological damage that comes from not being at peace with God, man, and the world.

We find that there is both an immediate and a culminating price to pay for present sin. There is also the eventual eternal payment which awaits those who stand before the final judgment seat of God. But there is also another adversity which will befall millions of unbelievers. This is an adversity unlike any the world has ever known (Matthew 24:21). Believers will be conspicuous by their absence during this time. It is a seven-year period of time known as "the great tribulation." During that time all unbelievers will try to hide from the wrath of God and will say to the mountains and the rocks, "Fall on us and hide us from the face of Him who sits on the throne and from the wrath of the Lamb! For the great day of His wrath has come, and who is able to stand?" (Rev. 6:16–17).

Unbelievers face more adversity than Christians do today; they have the unwelcome prospect of the Tribulation ahead of them, and they will suffer in hell for eternity. Will a Christian experience less adversity than an unbeliever? The answer must be "yes."

All of this does not minimize the real and present suffering and adversity that believers face in this world. Indeed, at times, we may wish to ask with the psalmist, "Lord, how long will the wicked triumph?" (Ps. 94:3; Rev. 6:10). Especially those who have been hurt by the evil deeds of men and women, and have not seen any outward retribution, will be prone to ask that question. However, it is not our place to cause them adversity in return or to even wish it upon them (Rom. 12:19; 1 Pet. 2:21–25; Matt. 5:38–48).

For our part, we should rejoice in the fact that God has forgiven us our sins. We will therefore come to a definite and glorious end to *all* adversity. Furthermore, we have been made new creatures with new natures. Our lives will be marked by less present adversity because they are devoted to God and because we reap what we sow. We know what it is to have God's kind of peace and to have joy in the inner man. We have experienced true Christian friendship and fellowship. We have the potential to love and to be loved in a way the world knows nothing of. The day of Tribulation will certainly come and perhaps come soon. "But you, brethren, are not in darkness, so that this Day should overtake you as a thief . . . for God did not appoint us to wrath, but to obtain salvation through our Lord Jesus Christ" (1 Thess. 5:4, 9).

Will a Christian experience less adversity than unbeliever? Yes! However, our goal is not to avoid all trials, but rather to grow and be strengthened by those we endure. As one poet so well expressed it:

> The tree that never had to fight
> For sun and sky and air and light,
> Never became a forest king,
> But lived and died a common thing.
> The man who never had to toil,
> Who never had to win his share
> Of sun and sky and light and air,
> Never became a manly man,
> But lived and died as he began.
> Good timber does not grow on ease.
> The stronger wind, the tougher trees,
> The farther sky, the greater length,
> By sun and cold, by rain and snow,
> In tree, or man, good timber grows.

Douglas Mallock

SHOULD WE PRAY FOR OR EXPECT OR DEMAND HEALING FOR SOMEONE WHO IS SERIOUSLY ILL?

The morning is the gate of day
But before you enter there
See that you set to guard it well
The sentinel of prayer

—Annie Johnson Flint

The answer to the above question would be "yes, maybe, and no." Yes, we should pray for healing. Whether or not we should "expect" healing depends on our definition of "expect." We should in no way demand healing. Much of the answer depends on our attitude. We must come before God with a heart full of faith, humility, submission to His will, and understanding of what He has revealed to us. We begin by being thankful that we can come to God in prayer and know that He hears and answers. I heard that there is a 900 prayer line for atheists: they call the number and nobody answers!

I have occasionally talked with believers who were uncertain of the propriety of praying for someone who was ill, whether it applied to themselves or someone they knew. Their objections centered around two questions: "Am I being selfish?" and "What if God intends for this person to be sick?"

Both questions are answered by humbly submitting to God's will. Since being well is a normal condition (at least for most people), asking to be well is not selfish or seeking what others do not normally have. If the person praying feels that it may be selfish, then he or she should make that very concern part of the prayer by saying something like, "Lord, I don't want to be selfish or self-seeking. I want most of all for Your will to be done. I have this concern for . . ."

Whether or not God intends for a person to be sick (as a chastisement or as a trial He has allowed or because He is taking them home) is a very difficult thing to discern. If there is such a question of God's intent, then the answer may well depend on what is accomplished in the person's life (how things work out). There are times when it is impossible for us to discern God's purposes; there are never times when we fear His purposes (Psalm 34:4). Ultimately, what makes prayer so meaningful for us is not that we connect with answers but that we connect with God.

That we should pray for someone who is ill (or facing any kind of difficulty) is readily apparent from the Scriptures. In a passage we have previously examined, Paul wrote: "Be anxious for nothing, but in everything by prayer and supplication, with thanksgiving, let your requests be made known to God" (Phil. 4:6). Notice in particular the inclusive words "nothing" and "everything." Surely illness fits in. We are invited by God to let our "requests be made known" to Him.

Another passage even more directly to the point is found in the book of James. There we read: "Is anyone among you suffering? Let him pray . . ." (James 5:13). That seems pretty straightforward. Perhaps the sickness is severe enough to cause some concern. Then what? "Is anyone among you sick? Let him call for the elders of the church, and let them pray over him, anointing him with oil in the name of the Lord" (James 5:14). In this case the elders of the church are summoned together for the purpose of both anointing and praying. The anointing is not magical nor does it have any medicinal value in this passage. Its purpose is well explained by Dr. Roy R. Roberts:[1]

> In brief, oil did have therapeutic value in ancient times as well as today, but it is best to understand it here as a symbol of God's miraculous work in healing.

That it had good medicinal effects is clear. It possessed soothing and curative value for animals, like sheep (Ps. 23:5), and men (Isa. 1:6). The good Samaritan in Christ's parable applied oil to the wounds of the man he helped (Luke 10:34). There are numerous instances of its use in extrabiblical sources (cf. Mayor, pp. 170ff; Mitton, p. 198; Plummer, p. 328). But it is not the meaning of James for various reasons. Though it was a therapeutic aid in some cases, it would not be a cure in all sicknesses in general. Further, James does not say in v. 15 that the oil will cure the sick or even that the oil plus the prayer will make him well. Specifically, he does say that "the prayer of faith shall save the sick," and makes no claim for the oil. It is not the oil but the Lord who "shall raise him up." There is also another factor. In the event that the oil were merely medicinal, would not one elder be sufficient to apply it, and not "elders" (plural)?

It is more adequate to say that the anointing is for the purpose of symbolizing tangibly the setting apart of the man to the miraculous healing work of God. It would be an aid to his faith by promoting a sense of expectancy. Christ Himself applied saliva to men at times evidently to symbolize, by physical contact, the healing that God would effect (Mark 7:33; 8:23). There is Old Testament support for the idea that the anointing could signify the setting apart of the man to God for His will and operation. There are numerous applications of oil not to cure but to set apart or identify things or persons with God in some sense. Jacob anointed the stone at Bethel to identify it as symbolizing the "house of God" in which he had been a guest (Gen. 28:1–8, 31:13). When he poured oil upon it, it was not to make it well! It was a ceremonial custom later to anoint priests (Exod. 18;41, 29;7; Lev. 8:12), prophets (1 Kgs. 19:16), and kings (1 Sam. 9:19, 10:1; 1 Kgs. 19:15). This was to symbolize that they were set apart to and identified with God for His will. When Jesus sent out the twelve disciples, they "anointed with oil many that were sick, and healed them" (Mark 6:13).

This is not just a ceremony of anointing with oil. The main ingredient is prayer. Much of the rest of the passage is devoted to showing the need for prayer mingled with faith, indeed, the "Elijah" kind of faith in praying. More directly related to our question as to whether we should pray is the instruction, "Confess your trespasses to one another, and pray for one another, that you may be healed" (Jas. 5:16). Again, it seems clear from these verses that it is not only proper to pray for an ill person, but we are *instructed* to do so.

The next question, namely, "Should we expect healing?" is a bit more difficult. As indicated earlier, the answer depends largely on what is meant by "expect." If we mean something like "I anticipate God's working" or "I know that God is faithful and His will is perfect," then the answer is "yes." If on the other hand, we mean something like "I *know* God is going to heal me," the answer may well be "no."

This may sound on the surface like an answer from weak faith. We should pray believing and we should ask in faith. But believing *what* and having faith in *what*? We are not to have faith in faith, as in "If I believe strong enough, this will happen." Faith in faith is idolatry. We are to have faith *only* in God. My faith in God is not that He will do *my* will but that He will faithfully perform His own will. My faith in God is not based on any promise that I would never know sickness or that I would be delivered from every sickness, but rather with Job, that "though He slay me, yet will I trust Him" (Job 13:15). If someone says he *knows* God is going to heal him, he presume to have God's knowledge (but see Isa. 55:8–9!). That is not faith, but presumption. In the case where someone says, "I know God will heal me," and he experiences healing (whether by medication, operation, or supernatural intervention), he might feel justified in saying, "See, I told you so." My answer would be that God fulfilled His will in his life and was gracious enough to allow him to be healed despite his presumption. I have also known personally of a number of cases where someone would say. "I know God is going to heal me," and yet it did not take place. This is an unfortunate circumstance where both the faith of the patient and the ability of God are called into question, especially by unbelievers.

The prayer of faith is not presumptuous. It trusts God to do what is right. It anticipates God's working (see chapter 11 of Part Two), all the while believing that *what* will be worked out or accomplished is God's will. The prayer of faith expects God to respond without dictating what that response will be.

The third part of the question, as to whether we should pray demanding healing, is answered with a definite "no." When I was in seminary I

worked part time in a factory. A co-worker claimed that "by His stripes
we are healed" (Isa. 53:5). This is, by the way, a beautiful passage describing how the Lord delivered us from our sins by His sacrifice and
brought spiritual healing (nothing is promised about physical healing).
This particular man and those of his persuasion were convinced that it
was contrary to God's will for them to be ill in any way. It was amusing,
but sad at times, to see him sneak off into a corner to blow his nose
because he refused to admit he had a cold. The leader of his church
(which also forbade any medical treatment and saw numerous people,
including babies, die) died at a relatively early age. His body was riddled
with several diseases. His followers predicted he would rise again the
third day. He didn't.

If anyone could have "demanded" or "claimed" healing based on a
godly life and active faith, it was the Apostle Paul. Yet we read that he
was plagued by "a thorn in the flesh" and that he "pleaded with the Lord
three times that it might depart" and God's answer was "no" (2 Cor.
12:7–9). God's will for Paul was that the affliction remain and that Paul
should learn and teach the sufficiency of God's grace. For Paul to demand
healing would be to demand other than God's will in his life. For Paul
to claim healing would be to claim more than God had promised.

Whether we get well or remain sick, whether we live or die, whether
we draw one more breath or ten million more, all is submitted to the
will of God (Jas. 4:13–16). It is our privilege to trust in God's goodness
and sovereignty for in that safe harbor we have an anchor steadfast and
sure.

Much of the propriety of what we ask the Lord is based on *how* we
ask the Lord. Our attitude is of great importance. We can all learn some
lessons from a leper who was healed by Jesus. His story is recorded in
this manner:

> When He had come down from the mountain, great multitudes fol-
> lowed Him. And behold, a leper came and worshipped Him, saying,
> "Lord, if You are willing, You can make me clean." Then Jesus put
> out His hand and touched him, saying, "I am willing; be cleansed."
> And immediately his leprosy was cleansed.
>
> (Matthew 8:1–3)

We can see five marks of his attitude in the second verse. First of all, he came to Jesus. The Lord wants us to come to Him with our problems. Sometimes pride will prevent us. Humility and a recognition of our need bring us to Jesus. Secondly, we find that the leper "worshipped Him." We must come to Jesus in an attitude of worship and a heart filled with adoration for who He is and for what He has done. Truly, He is worthy! Thirdly, he recognized the lordship of Jesus by calling Him "Lord." He is not just our Savior, He is our Lord. He is not just our good buddy, He is the holy God. An attitude that recognizes the awesomeness of God's majesty and holiness makes no demands and strikes no deals (Isa. 6:1–7). Fourth, the leper subjected his request to the will of the Lord by saying, "if you are willing." There is nothing more important that could happen in our lives than the will of God. Lastly, there is a statement of faith: "You can make me clean." His expectation was not that Jesus *had* to do it nor that He certainly *would* do it. His hope and expectation was that the Lord, who was worthy of his worship and praise and submission, had the power and ability even to take away his leprosy. The response of Jesus, of course, was, "I am willing; be cleansed."

We should indeed pray. As we pray, may our faith be in God and may our attitude be one of worship, humility, submission and trust.

IF "THE END OF OUR LIFE IS IN GOD'S HANDS," WHY SEEK HELP?

The first thing we must determine is if this is a true statement: the end of our life is in God's hands. In other words, does God just *know* when we are going to die (since He is all-knowing) or does He *determine* when we are going to die (since He is sovereign over all)? If God only *knows*, then the statement is false. If God both knows and determines, then the statement is true.

God is not just a spectator who sits in heaven watching from a distance and already knowing the outcome. We would have very little comfort if all we could say about God is that He knows what will happen. When Paul wrote to the Thessalonians about the dead in Christ and the rapture, he concluded with "Therefore comfort one another with these words" (1 Thess. 4:18). Why could there be comfort? Because God not only knows what will happen, He has determined what will happen. As Paul went on to describe the coming of the Lord as a thief in the night, he concluded with "Therefore comfort each other and edify one another . . ." (1 Thess 5:11). How could there be comfort? Because "God did not appoint us to wrath, but to obtain salvation through our Lord Jesus Christ" (1 Thess. 5:9). God did not just *know*, He *appointed* or *determined* what would happen. God does not sit around waiting to see what will happen. He knows because He has determined; therefore,

177

He often speaks in the past tense of future events (see, for instance, Rom. 8:29–30). He performs His will. As Paul said, ". . . we have obtained an inheritance, being predestined according to the purpose of Him who works all things according to the counsel of His will" (Eph. 1:11).

Perhaps the clearest statement on this subject is found in the Psalms. David wrote: "Your eyes saw my substance, being yet unformed. And in Your book they all were written, the days fashioned for me, when as yet there were none of them" (Ps. 139:16). God not only knows but he "fashioned" our entire life-span.

Now that we have determined that the statement is true, i.e., the end of our life is in God's hands, what do we do and how do we respond? One approach is fatalism. In this approach the person gives up. Why fight against something already set and unavoidable? This person would say "It's just my fate." The problem with fatalism is that it leads to lack of hope. We must remember that our life is not in the hands of fate or blind chance. Our lives are in God's hands! That is the *only* place where there is genuine hope. Instead of fatalism, I would suggest that our situation is just the opposite. We have great hope because of "determinism." *God* has determined. He knows best; He has absolute power; He is perfect in all his ways and works, and what He has determined to be best for my life is just that—best for my life. I am not up against blind chance or fate; I am completely in His loving care. There is no safer spot.

Returning now to the original question (if the end of our life is in God's hands, why seek help?), we could counter with the simple question: Why not? What would be the *purpose* of not seeking help? Is there any benefit in not seeking help?

If I did not eat, I would become ill. If I went long enough without eating, my illness would become terminal. But, as some would ask, if the end of my life is in God's hands, why seek help? I have never met anyone who asked that question and yet refused to eat. When they became hungry, rather than become ill and eventually die, they ate. When we become ill, rather than let that illness progress to the point where we may eventually die from it, we should seek help. We have no problem applying this idea to hunger. In fact, we tend to over-apply it! To not apply it to illness reveals a basic inconsistency. We could examine any number of illustrations. For example, if a train was about to run over me, why move (since the end of my life is in God's hands)? Yet, I trust we all would make the right decision to move out of harm's way. It reminds us of Satan's temptation of Jesus when he challenged Jesus to cast himself off of the pinnacle of the temple. Satan assured Jesus that God would watch over him. The Lord's answer was "It is written again, 'You shall not tempt the Lord your God'" (Matt. 4:7).

The Lord expects us to use good sense and to seek help as it is needed. The first place we go for help is to the Lord Himself. In a Psalm written by Asaph we read this invitation: "Call upon Me in the day of trouble; I will deliver you, and you shall glorify Me" (Psalm 50:15). God wants us to seek His help. We must recognize our dependence upon Him. The two results listed in this verse are our deliverance and God's glory. This brings up an interesting point, in that our well-being is not the only consideration. How does our illness or problem affect God's glory? Why seek help? Not only for our good but for God's glory. We need to be able to pray as the Norwegian theologian Ole Hallesby did: "Lord, if it will be to Your glory, heal suddenly. If it will glorify You more, heal gradually; if it will glorify You even more, may your servant remain sick awhile; and if it glorify Your name still more, take him to Yourself in heaven."[2]

As demonstrated in the last chapter of Part Two, we need to seek to help ourselves. Prayer is first, but putting feet to those prayers is a close second. Doctors report that it is the person who gives up who is most likely to die. Those who fight back and have a will to live and get better have a much better chance of doing just that. Some of us just give up too easily. I read the story of a fortune-teller who studied the hand of a young man and said, "You will be poor and very unhappy until you are thirty-seven years old." The young man responded, "Well, after that, what will happen? Will I be rich and happy?" the fortune-teller said, "No, you'll still be poor, but you'll be used to it after that."

We should also accept the help of others and seek to help others. It is abundantly clear that the Lord expects us to have such a response. The Lord holds up to us the example of the good Samaritan. Even more direct are the words through John that "Whoever has this world's goods, and sees his brother in need, and shuts up his heart from him, how does the love of God abide in him?" (1 John 3:17). James asks a similar question: "If a brother or sister is naked and destitute of daily food, and one of you says to them, 'Depart in peace, be warmed and filled,' but you do not give them the things which are needed for the body, what does it profit?" (James 2:15–16).

For many of us, it is more difficult to accept help than to give help. Pride gets in the way. We don't want to rely on anyone but ourselves. To admit a need is to admit a failure or at least a weakness (or so we believe). I struggled with that for the first five years of my Christian life. Finally, a dear brother said just one sentence which changed my perspective. He said, "There is a grace to receiving just as there is a grace to giving." I guess I had been ungracious in my receiving. If God has asked His people to minister to one another, shouldn't the one being ministered to be gracious? If one person is fulfilling the will of God in giving, should the other person refuse the will of God by not receiving? God will bless the person who gives. The person who refuses to accept the aid runs the risk of robbing the giver of a blessing.

The times when someone in our churches need to *ask* for help should be few. We should be on the lookout for opportunities to give and to minister to one another. We need to develop sensitive hearts. We need to keep an eye open for possible opportunities to be used of God in helping our brothers and sisters. As a pastor, I rejoice in having some folks in our congregation who seek chances to serve in such a way. Some of them do it totally behind the scenes—serving and helping out in unknown and unseen and unheralded ways (except to God!). Others help me by bringing particular needs they have learned of to my attention. This is helpful because it is impossible for me to keep close track of everyone. Discretion, of course, is essential in such cases. The key is to be sensitive and to seek to minister.

The end of our life and every day in between is in the Lord's hands. We move forward, not with a fatalistic attitude, but with a victorious viewpoint, seeking help when it is needed and seeking to help when and where we can.

ARE "FAITH HEALERS" FOR REAL?

A young woman came to me unsure of what to do. She was at that time suffering from a malady (not serious) and had received in the mail an offer of help. A certain "minister," who proclaimed himself to be a "healer," was willing to pray for her healing. Great!—Except for a couple of problems. First of all, he wanted her to send back to him a handkerchief. The purpose of the handkerchief was mysterious and reminds one more of occult practices than biblical healing. Along with the handkerchief, she was to send a minimum "donation" of ten dollars. Later, I discovered from other sources that the ten dollars was just a beginning. To "keep healthy" the "donations" had to keep flowing in.

I was able to convince my friend not to be involved or to even respond. I assured her that I and many others would be glad to pray for free. An even more important consideration was whether this practice and the whole idea of faith healing was biblical, or not. The question is complicated by the fact that God *did* give "gifts of healings" (1 Cor. 12:9). But does that apply today? If not, why not? A sincere desire to *be* healed also clouds the issue. We may tend to grasp at straws and refuse to look at the issue biblically and objectively. The question is not, "What do I want?" nor is it "What do they promise or claim?" The question to ask is "What saith the Lord?"

It is helpful to investigate the Lord's purpose for the gifts of healings (and other sign gifts for that matter) to help determine if that purpose is still operative. It might appear that the obvious purpose for the gifts of healings was to remove illness. I would suggest that that was more a *benefit* than a purpose. If that was the purpose, we would certainly wonder why only certain people were healed and why only in certain time periods.

The Lord Himself has revealed the purpose of the sign gifts. Sign gifts (to which category the gifts of healings belong) were given, as their name suggests, as a sign. They were always used to authenticate new revelation from God.

This purpose for such supernatural signs was not confined to the New Testament. The clearest indication of the authenticating purpose of sign gifts in the Old Testament is found in the calling of Moses as God's spokesman.

> Then Moses answered and said, "But suppose they will not believe me or listen to my voice; suppose they say, 'The Lord has not appeared to you.'" So the Lord said to him, "What is that in your hand?" He said, "A rod." And He said, "Cast it on the ground." So he cast it on the ground, and it became a serpent; and Moses fled from it. Then the Lord said to Moses, "Reach out your hand and take it by the tail" (and he reached out his hand and caught it, and it became a rod in his hand). "That they may believe that the Lord God of their fathers, the God of Abraham, the God of Isaac, and the God of Jacob, has appeared to you." Furthermore the Lord said to him, "Now put your hand in your bosom." And he put his hand in his bosom, and when he took it out, behold, his hand was leprous, like snow. And He said, "Put your hand in your bosom again." So he put his hand in his bosom again, and drew it out of his bosom, and behold, it was restored like his other flesh. "Then it will be, if they do not believe you, nor heed the message of the first sign, that they may believe the message of the latter sign. "And it shall be, if they do not believe even these two signs, or listen to your voice, that you shall take water from the river and pour it on the dry land. And the water which you take from the river will become blood on the dry land."

Notice in verse one that the concern of Moses was how to prove or demonstrate that the revelation was from God. The Lord demonstrated to Moses the kind of supernatural power that He would use through Moses to authenticate the message. The purpose of the serpent was not to teach us to handle serpents. The purpose of the leprous hand made well again was not to teach us how to heal leprosy. Nor did Moses go around healing lepers—that was not the purpose of this sign. The purpose, as stated by God, was "that they may believe that the Lord God of their fathers, the God of Abraham, the God of Isaac, and the God of Jacob, has appeared to you" (Exod. 4:5).

In the Gospels, Jesus repeatedly pointed to His supernatural works as signs that He was the Messiah (John 4:48, 5:36, 6:30). In Peter's sermon on the Day of Pentecost we read: "Men of Israel, hear these words: Jesus of Nazareth, a Man attested by God to you by miracles, wonders and signs which God did though Him in your midst, as you yourselves also know . . ." (Acts 2:22). The point is, if Jesus is who He claimed to be (and He is!), then we ought to give very close attention to what He says. One of the ways He has shown who He is, is by His works. They were signs to authenticate Him and His message. He was "attested by God" and the way that was accomplished was "by miracles, wonders, and signs . . ."

When the Apostles prayed for boldness to preach, they also prayed for the accompanying signs to authenticate the message. This would be new revelation to the Jews (that Jesus was God, etc.) and the Jews always wanted signs (1 Cor. 1:22). Notice their prayer:

> Now, Lord, look on their threats, and grant to Your servants that with all boldness they may speak Your word, by stretching out Your hand to heal, and that signs and wonders may be done through the name of Your holy Servant Jesus. And when they had prayed, the place where they were assembled together was shaken; and they were all filled with the Holy Spirit, and they spoke the word of God with boldness.
>
> (Acts 4:29–31)

We see the same thing in the ministry of Paul. As he wrote to the Romans:

Nevertheless, brethren, I have written more boldly to you on some points, as reminding you, because of the grace given to me by God, that I might be a minister of Jesus Christ to the Gentiles, ministering the gospel of God, that the offering of the Gentiles might be acceptable, sanctified by the Holy Spirit. Therefore I have reason to glory in Christ Jesus in the things which pertain to God. For I will not dare to speak of any of those things which Christ has not accomplished through me, in word and deed, to make the Gentiles obedient—in mighty signs and wonders, by the power of the Spirit of God, so that from Jerusalem and round about to Illyricum I have fully preached the gospel of Christ.

(Romans 15:15–19)

The writer of Hebrews spoke of the new revelation proclaimed by Christ and by those who heard Him. This revelation centered around "so great a salvation" (Heb. 2:3). The writer goes on to say: "God also bearing witness both with signs and wonders, with various miracles, and gifts of the Holy Spirit, according to His own will" (Heb. 2:4).

The conclusion is that the stated purpose of God in giving supernatural sign gifts (such as healing) was to demonstrate His involvement and thus to authenticate the new revelation. The question then arises concerning this connection: If God has finished giving new revelation (which almost every believer will affirm is true—God having ended revelation with the completion of the New Testament), and if the stated purpose of sign gifts (such as healing) was to authenticate new revelation, then should we expect there to be faith healers today? The answer must be "no."

It is interesting to note that in the four New Testament passages where spiritual gifts are mentioned (1 Corinthians 12; Romans 12; 1 Peter 4; Ephesians 4), sign gifts are listed *only* in 1 Corinthians. This may be the case because 1 Corinthians was written *before* the other books. It is likely that even before the completion of the New Testament the sign gifts were beginning to diminish and thus they are not even mentioned in the later books of the New Testament. For example, in Paul's last letter before his death, he wrote: ". . . Trophimus I have left in Miletus sick" (2 Tim. 4:20). God used Paul as an avenue of healing to many in the beginning of his ministry (see Acts 19:11–20 for example), yet we do not read of Paul healing others later in his ministry. Rather, he gave Timothy the advice to "use a little wine for your stomach's sake and your frequent infirmities" (1 Tim. 5:23) and had to leave Trophimus behind because he was sick. As the new revelation (New Testament) neared completion, so did the sign gifts that had been used to authenticate it (1 Cor. 13:8–10).

Going back to the example of my friend, how does the letter, the solicitation, the handkerchief, and the money involved in today's faith healing correspond with the biblical pattern? Not every "faith healer" uses a handkerchief or the same methods; but we should ask: does what they *do* use, match up with the Bible? What does slapping someone in the forehead and yelling "heal!" have to do with biblical healing? What role does faith play and *who* is to have faith?

When we examine the biblical references to healing we find that they had the following characteristics: they were instant, obvious, complete, never failed, undeniable, not for gain (*never* was money solicited, in fact, just the opposite was the case), and they were used to bring exclusive glory to God (never to man). Several notable passages to check, besides the healings of Jesus, are Acts 3:1–13, 4:13–16, 14:8–18. Compare these with "healings" today which are often protracted, uncertain, partial, and sometimes failures. The "healer" may wear a diamond ring, drive an expensive car, and bring glory to himself. Money is always solicited. No, "faith healers" are not for real.

For healing to take place, *who* is to have the faith? Modern faith healers always put the burden on the person needing to be healed. They say, "You did not get healed because you did not believe enough!" It seems ironic that they would label themselves as *faith* healers and yet demand that the faith come from the sick person and not themselves.

Although Jesus did from time to time point to someone's faith as being instrumental in bringing about their healing (see, for example, Matt. 9:18–22), that was not always the case. The lame man brought by his four friends (Mark 2:1–12) was not said to have exercised any faith. It was the faith of his friends which moved Jesus to action (Mark 2:5). The man born blind (John 9) did not exercise faith. The lame man healed by Peter (Acts 3) asked for alms, not healing, and exercised no faith since he was unaware of what God was about to do. Lazarus

(John 11) exercised no faith as he was raised from the dead! I believe that faith must *always* be present. It is not always present in the person healed, but it is always present in the healer.

There is supernatural healing going on today. If not, there would be no reason to pray! The question is not "is there healing?" but "*who* is the faith healer?" That question is answered for us by James. In the passage where he speaks of the elders coming at the request of the sick person to anoint and pray, he says: "And the prayer of faith will save the sick and the Lord will raise him up . . ." (James 5:15). The elders should come, anoint, pray, and have faith, but it is "the Lord" who has the power to raise up that sick individual. We are not denying supernatural healing. We are simply saying that the *Lord* is the "faith healer."

Since the biblically stated purpose of sign miracles (such as healing) is not in usage today (there being no new revelation to authenticate), and since the "healing" going on today bears little resemblance to New Testament healing, and since the ceasing of such gifts was prophesied (and apparently began taking place even before the New Testament was completed), we can conclude that modern "faith healers" are not for real. Do not mail them back a handkerchief; do not send them money, and do not rely upon them.

Jesus is the faith healer. Submit yourself and your need to Him. Ask others to pray for you, but don't pay anyone to do it. Have faith in God, not man. The Lord Himself can and does mightily heal. It is according to His purpose and plan. It is in keeping with His timing. We can rest assured that it is by His wisdom, in His love, in demonstration of His power and for His glory that He chooses to heal or not to heal. Trust Him.

WILL MODERN SCIENCE & MEDICINE EVER WIPE OUT SICKNESS?

G reat strides forward have been made in recent years in the areas of science and medicine. I heard one scientist say that he could easily spend all his time just reading journals, reports, and books describing and discussing advancements in modern technology and he would still be behind! Advancements in the area of medicine are nothing to sneeze at, either. We all applaud the improvements—many of us have been helped by them personally. I have a heart problem which my cardiologist informed me could not be improved by operation. A new heart surgeon moved into our area, heard of my case, and offered to perform a new surgical technique on my heart. He drilled nineteen holes through my heart with a laser! It worked wonderfully and now I have a "holey" heart! This surgeon, Dr. Clay Burnett, is a strong believer in Christ and a uniquely gifted individual. We can be grateful for doctors like him, we encourage research and we look forward to new breakthroughs. Where, however, is all this going to lead? Will modern science and medicine ever wipe out sickness?

If you have moved in recent years, you have probably been faced with the same problem I had—trying to find a doctor. It isn't that there is a shortage of doctors. In fact, there are *more* doctors in practice now than in previous years. Part of the problem may be attributed to population growth. This, however, would account for only a small portion since we have one of the lowest birth rates in the world and our population in most areas is not increasing at a rapid pace. The answer is that people are still getting sick. Not only are we still plagued with the standard colds, flus, and viruses, but we are from time to time informed of new strains which seem harder to treat and are more devastating to the body. Problems with more serious concerns, such as cancer and heart disease, seem rampant. We have come a long way in medicine but we have not come close to wiping out medical problems.

It is hard to conceive how sick a world we live in. If the advancements in modern medicine had *not* been made, imagine where we would be now! If all we had was the medical technology of fifty years ago, many more lives would be lost to the battle of disease, and they would be lost much quicker. We are not stopping the flood; we are just bailing with a new, improved bucket.

There is no possibility of modern science and medicine ever eliminating sickness. I do not say this to discredit doctors or scientists, for I have great admiration for their talents and achievements. The reason I can be so definite (pessimistic, if you prefer) is because of the testimony of Scripture. We find in the Bible that sickness is related to judgment and that judgment is determined by God, and not by man. Note, I am not saying that sickness is always or necessarily directly related to personal sin (see Part One, Reasons 1 and 2). Sickness can, however, be traced to God's judgment. We find that to be true in at least four areas: the original curse, chastisement of believers, current punishment of nonbelievers, and the coming Tribulation.

Sickness is a result of the original curse. Because of sin, man was cursed and the whole planet we live on was cursed. The curse has not yet been repealed. As long as the curse is in existence, sickness will be in the world. No amount of research, effort, medical advances, or medicines will alter that fact. This is indeed a bleak outlook and it reminds us of Paul's words: "If in this life only we have hope in Christ, we are of all men most pitiable" (1 Cor. 15:19).

Sickness may also be the result of God's chastisement of His children (Hebrews 12:5–11). Our Father does not give up on us, and as long as we are in this world He will continue to mold us to the image of His

Son. That process will from time to time involve chastisement. This chastisement may take the form of sickness. If that is the case, there is no way that man will ever keep or deter God in the slightest from dealing with His own children according to His will.

Another reason that sickness will never be wiped out is because of God's current punishment of nonbelievers. This punishment comes in both direct and indirect forms. An example of direct punishment is the unenviable sickness and subsequent death of King Herod. Because he accepted the crowd's praise of "the voice of a god and not of a man," an angel of the Lord struck him "and he was eaten by worms and died" (Acts 12:22–23). An example of indirect punishment is found in Proverbs 23:29–35 which speaks of the ill effects of consuming alcoholic drinks. God does not directly intervene in such cases, but rather lets the sinner suffer from the results of his own sin. In either case, punishment is due. Man and science will never be able to stay the hand of a righteous God. An ant walking on a railroad track has more chance of derailing a train than all of mankind with all their discoveries and efforts have of keeping God from inflicting sickness on those He would punish.

Besides the current punishment, there is a time of Tribulation yet to come which will last for seven years and will be characterized as ". . . great tribulation, such as has not been since the beginning of the world until this time, no, nor ever shall be" (Matt. 24:21). Even though this is a *future* event and by then perhaps more discoveries will have been made in both scientific and medical technology, man still will not have eliminated sickness. An example of the plagues that will face mankind is found in Revelation 16. There we read: "And they blasphemed the God of heaven because of their pains and their sores, and did not repent of their deeds" (Rev. 16:11). Two items stand out in this verse. One is the reaction of those who are plagued. These are comprised of those ". . . who had the mark of the beast and those who worshipped his image" (Rev. 16:2). That they are confirmed in their wickedness is demonstrated by the fact that they blasphemed God and refused to repent. This is striking when we realize that they will know that the plagues are from God and that He alone has power over these plagues (Rev. 16:9). In light of that, it is impossible to think that man will ever wipe out sickness. Man may make some progress in fighting a limited number of diseases, but he will never overcome them all. In addition, we read very clearly that "God . . . has power over these plagues" (Rev. 16:9), not scientists, not doctors, not man, and not Satan.

The question was, "Will modern science and medicine ever wipe out sickness?" The answer to that question must be a definite "no." But if we rephrase the question to "Will sickness ever be wiped out?" we can answer "yes." When God makes a new heaven and a new earth, He "will wipe away every tear from their eyes; there shall be no more pain, for the former things have passed away" (Rev. 21:4). We also read that in the New Jerusalem ". . . there shall be no more curse . . ." (Rev. 22:3). God will bring a definite and glorious end to sickness.

Again we are brought to the inescapable conclusion that our hope and trust are not to be in man, but in God. We do not look for what man might do, but for what God *will* do. To Him be the glory!

How Can I Be a Testimony to Others When I Don't Feel Well?

It's not too difficult to have a good testimony when all is going well. The metal is not tested until the heat is applied. The person who seems victorious one day can appear crushed by defeat the very next day. Too often our testimonies are like roller coasters; they reflect vast fluctuations as we move through life. We sense that our reactions and our testimonies should be more even and that they should remain at a high and proper level regardless of external circumstances. Not only is that tough to accomplish, but it's a bit like expecting a captain to grin as he sinks with his vessel. We are constantly confronted with the problem of being a good testimony to others even when we just do not feel like it.

One of our main problems is that we have not rightly understood what it means to be a good testimony. Does being a good testimony mean that we should never cry, especially not in public? If that were so, what would we say about Jesus, who wept openly at the death of his friend Lazarus, who wept over the city of Jerusalem, and who wept in the garden? Not only do we have His example, but we also have the instruction to "Rejoice with those who rejoice, and weep with those who weep" (Romans 12:15). In fact, it would seem that the person who refuses to weep would have the poorer testimony, since they could be viewed as being callous and hard-hearted. We would suspect the sanity of the captain who grinned as his vessel sank.

Being a good testimony does not mean that we just grin and bear it. It does not mean that calamity does not touch us or that we cannot feel the hurt of others. A good testimony means that we *rightly* respond to circumstances with the correct measure of caring and trust.

We need to realize that it is *okay* not to feel well at times. There is nothing wrong with feeling pain when we hit our thumb with a hammer. Our reaction to that pain, i.e., *what* we say and *how* we say it, is the crucial point. It is normal to cry out in pain (believe me, I have carried out this experiment numerous times with the same results). Cursing, on the other hand, is a poor testimony. The problem is not that we feel pain but how we respond to it.

Pride can prevent us from responding correctly to pain in our lives. I remember my first day on the job as a service technician. My boss and I were sitting on the floor repairing a piece of communications equipment and there was a hot soldering iron on the floor between us. Having made the necessary repairs, we both started to get up. I placed my hand on top of the hot iron as I was getting up. I heard a sizzle, smelled something burning and felt the pain right away. My boss, who had his back to me at that moment, asked if I smelled something burning. I sniffed around in the air and said, "Yes, I think I do." I didn't tell him *what* was burning. I saw no use in adding insult to injury. Pride caused me to conceal my pain. So it is with a lot of our hurts; we are really more concerned about our pride than we are about our Christian testimony.

Wrong theology can also prevent us from responding correctly. Those who believe that Christians should not have health problems place themselves in quite a quandary when those inevitable problems come. Also, those who view God as a servant (instead of the other way around) may respond in anger or frustration that God would not take better care of them. These views lead to testimonies which reflect an inaccurate understanding of God and His ways. Consequently, deficient theology makes it even more difficult to maintain a proper testimony in the face of adversity.

King David was willing to admit when he was overwhelmed with trials. His open and frank cries for help were on public record and even put to music. One song which may very well have been at the top of the music charts in Israel is recorded for us in Psalm 40. The last half of that song goes like this:

> Do not withhold Your tender mercies from me, O Lord; Let Your lovingkindness and Your truth continually preserve me. For innumerable evils have surrounded me; My iniquities have overtaken me, so that I am not able to look up; They are more than the hairs of my head; Therefore my heart fails me. Be pleased, O Lord, to deliver me; O Lord, make haste to help me! Let them be ashamed and brought to mutual confusion who seek to destroy my life; Let them be driven backward and brought to dishonor who wish me evil. Let them be confounded because of their shame, who say to me, "Aha, aha!"
> Let all those who seek You rejoice and be glad in You; Let such as love Your salvation say continually, "The Lord be magnified!" But I am poor and needy; Yet the Lord thinks upon me. You are my help and my deliverer; Do not delay, O my God.
>
> (Psalm 40:11–17)

David had a good testimony, not because all was well and he was smiling, not because all was not well and he was still smiling, but because, even though he might say "I am not able to look up" and "my heart fails me," he could sing of God: "You are my help and my deliverer."

The first step in being a good testimony, even when we do not feel like it, is to realize that it is okay not to feel well; it is proper to acknowledge pain. Having recognized the need, we must then truly commit both ourselves and that need to God.

Our testimony, after all, is not that we are without problems or that problems do not affect us. Our testimony is that we have a God who is much bigger than our problems. Therefore, the proper testimony is that we are committing ourselves and our problems to Him. This removes the basis of our testimony from "how we feel" to "who God is."

The degree to which we will actually be able to live that testimony will be determined by our level of trust. We cannot be standing on the solid Rock and riding the roller coaster at the same time. Someone in the roller coaster may *wish* he were on solid ground, but until he get off the roller coaster he will experience the fluctuations inherent in that ride. It is not those who *wish* they were standing on the solid Rock, but those who *are* standing there that live a consistent, godly testimony.

Having acknowledged the problem and then having committed it to God, we need to continue on to magnify the Lord. We magnify the Lord when all is well, and there is no reason to cease because there are problems. In the Psalm we looked at earlier, David said: "Let all those who seek You rejoice and be glad in You; let such as love Your salvation say continually, the Lord be magnified" (Ps. 40:16). Note the word "continually"—in good times as well as bad.

We magnify the Lord by giving Him the praise, honor, and respect that He is due. It is hard to praise God and complain at the same time. Making Him the center of our focus, which is where He should be (see Part Two, Response one), displaces our focus on the problem. This in itself does not remove the problem, but rather, grants us the right perspective of it.

We can have a good testimony even when we don't feel well by acknowledging our need, by committing that need and ourselves to God, by seeking to magnify the Lord at all times and by asking God to enable us to have a good testimony.

Since our testimony may well reflect the character of our Lord to the unsaved, we want to make sure that they get a correct picture. Our Lord is even more concerned than we are about the glory of His name. Recognizing that we have the possibility (if not the propensity!) of displaying a poor testimony, we should pray for divine enablement to respond in a godly way and to demonstrate our trust in God despite the adversity.

God will lift those up who trust in Him. We can say with David: "Why are you cast down, O my soul? And why are you disquieted within me? Hope in God; for I shall yet praise Him, the help of my countenance and my God" (Psalm 43:5).

It is possible to be a good testimony even when we do not feel well, but the basis of that testimony must be founded not on our feelings, but on God's faithfulness. The focus of our attention must not be on our adversity, but on our Lord. Our testimony is not that we don't cry, but that we cry to our Father and we know that He hears and He cares. Such a testimony stands in any storm.

WHAT ABOUT LIFE-SUPPORT SYSTEMS AND EUTHANASIA?

There are times when we have the awesome and painful task of making a decision as to whether someone lives or dies. The decision is complicated by the fact that the person's life we are considering is very precious to us, a spouse, a parent, a loved one. The desire to cling to life, the dread of guilt, the hopelessness we feel and the sorrow we share for that suffering loved one are all emotional responses which cloud our thinking. There are other considerations, such as the enormous cost of continued treatment and the physical and emotional trauma of those who are watching their loved one slip away. At this point, a doctor comes to us with a question: "Do you desire life-support systems to be used?" Even if this question is not posed to us, a thought may enter our thinking: "Should I put an end to the suffering?"

The first question has to do with life-support systems. We will seek to give some guidelines for answering that question later. The second question has to do with euthanasia, which is sometimes termed "mercy killing."

In a poll conducted in early 1990, 80% of those surveyed said decisions about ending the lives of terminally ill patients who cannot decide for themselves should be made by their families and doctors rather than lawmakers. If the patient is terminally ill and unconscious but has left instructions in a living will, 81% believe the doctor should be allowed to withdraw life-sustaining treatment; 57% believe it is all right for doctors in such cases to go even further and administer lethal injections or provide lethal pills.[3]

Euthanasia is the bringing about of someone's death in an easy and painless way in order to relieve their suffering. The word itself is derived from two Greek words, the first word *eu* meaning "good" and the second word *thanatos* meaning "death." It is a qualitative idea—causing a "good death" instead of allowing a "bad death." The term "mercy killing" is also used. The French word for "mercy" is *misericorde*. This same word was used of a narrow dagger employed in medieval times to deliver the death stroke to a seriously wounded knight.[4]

Euthanasia, or mercy killing, should never be considered as an option. It is the deliberate taking of another person's life, otherwise known as murder, and we know that God has clearly stated: "you shall not murder" (Exodus 20:13).

Mercy killing is a crime which is seldom fully prosecuted. In fact, out of some 20 U.S. cases of mercy killings in the past 50 years, only three defendants have been sentenced to jail.[5] However, the question for us is not what is acceptable legally or socially, but what is acceptable biblically.

There is an interesting account of the death of King Saul which serves as a good illustration. Saul and his army were badly beaten by the Philistines. Saul was severely wounded by the archers. He told his armorbearer: "Draw your sword, and thrust me through with it, lest these uncircumcised men come and thrust me through and abuse me" (1 Samuel 31:4). Saul was asking for his armorbearer to perform a mercy killing. The armorbearer refused to do it so Saul committed suicide. The armorbearer then followed his master's example. The story does not end there. In the next book we read of an Amalekite who presented himself to David as the one who ended Saul's life. He reported that Saul had begged: "Please stand over me and kill me, for anguish has come upon me, but my life still remains in me" (2 Sam. 1:9). The Amalekite lied, of course, probably thinking he would be favorably looked upon as having done a favor for both Saul and David. He even brought Saul's crown to David—surely there would be a great reward! The reward the man received was to lose his own life (2 Sam. 1:14–16).

Euthanasia is never an option. Life-support systems, however, may be an option. In determining whether or not to consider it, we must remember that each case is different. There are so many variables (people, disease, chances of recovery, spiritual condition, etc.) that there can be no pat answers. All we can do is suggest some principles and ways of thinking through the decision. In the end, each person is accountable for and responsible for his own decision. No one can make that decision for you, and we certainly do not propose to do that here.

Lewis Smedes struck a good balance when he wrote: "I believe that in our decision making we must have a passion for life, but a compassion for the living."[6] The Bible does not directly address the issue, but there are two biblical principles which sometimes seem to come into tension with one another: the sanctity of life (Genesis 9:3–6) and compassion for others. We support and acknowledge both principles. Consider a case, however, in which a loved one is terminally ill and in great pain. When the option of life-support systems is given, if you lean toward the sanctity of life, you will likely accept, but if you lean toward compassion for others, you will likely refuse. This is by no means to say that a person who refuses the life-support systems has no compassion nor that one who acts out of compassion does not hold dear the sanctity of life. In fact, that is the very reason there is a problem in making the decision—we want both, and that is the point of Smedes' statement.

There are some things we can do to help minimize this tension. One of the most important steps to take is a preventative one. Decide beforehand what the family should do. I, for instance, have given clear instructions to my family concerning my own desires in the event that such a decision has to be made. This not only helps them to decide, but also helps to alleviate feelings of guilt. The best time to talk over such decisions is before they are upon us and before the natural emotional reactions cloud the issue. Forty states have living-will laws that allow people to specify in advance what treatments they would find acceptable in their final days.

In a case where a decision or request has not been made known beforehand, we need a way of thinking through the options. As Dr. Elkins said, "The Lord has allowed us to develop the technologies of today, and it is our responsibility to use them in a framework of Christian principles." [7]

I would like to suggest a test consisting of three questions. If you can answer "yes" to all three questions, then you might want to consider and pray about the option of not using life-support systems. If you answer "no" to any question, you should probably use life-support.

The first question is: "Is the person saved?" If the answer is yes, we know that the person's death would be a promotion into the very presence of the Lord. If, however, the answer is no, then we know that the person's death would usher them into an eternal state where "the worm does not die and the thirst is not quenched" (Mark 9:48). There is no returning from that place and no chance of being saved from its torment once the gates of death have been shut (Luke 16:19–26). No matter how great their suffering may appear to be in this present life, it holds no comparison to that which will be their lot in death. As long as they are on this side of death, there is still hope that they might be saved and escape the punishment which they (and we!) deserve.

The second question to ask is: "Is the situation hopeless?" At this point you will likely be at the mercy of doctors. Doctors are well-trained experts, but they are not infallible. It would be wise to get a second or even a third opinion.

The Rev. Harry Cole, a Presbyterian minister, faced this difficult decision when his wife, Jackie, fell into a coma. A massive brain hemorrhage left Mrs. Cole in a vegetative state, which doctors said could last indefinitely. After consulting with his family, Cole went to court to have the respirator removed. Circuit Court Judge Byrnes stayed his decision. Six days later, Jackie Cole woke up. She suffers some short-term memory loss, but otherwise, is fully recovered.[8]

I have found a number of physicians unwilling to give any definite answers. Perhaps they are so tentative because of the legal and financial ramifications—they might be sued if they are wrong. This mutual lack of trust serves only to hurt everyone involved.

If there is a strong indication that the situation is hopeless, you should ask: "What is the *purpose* of continuing?" There may be a good, legitimate purpose or reason. I am just suggesting that you ask the question.

If, on the other hand, it is not certain that the situation is hopeless, perhaps you should seriously consider doing whatever it takes to preserve that life. The Child Abuse Amendment of 1984 included the "Baby Doe" provisions. Part of this section says: "The law makes it a criminal offense not to treat certain infants, except in those cases where the infant's condition would make any type of medical treatment futile or where treatment would simply prolong the death process."[9] We are bound scripturally, morally, and legally to do what we can. If there is not hope (apparent), that does not mean we *cannot* provide treatment. If there is hope, that means we cannot withhold treatment.

The third question is: "Is my response passive?" An example of an *active* response would be euthanasia—purposefully killing the individual. In such a case, your answer to the question (is my response passive?) would have to be "no." As mentioned earlier in this chapter, this is a solution unacceptable to God.

Refusing life-support systems, however, may be considered a passive response. Remember that by this time you should have already determined that the person is saved and that the situation is hopeless. That is why this question comes last. If the person is saved, you have nothing to lose spiritually. If the situation is hopeless, you have nothing to lose physically. The individual is in God's hands and care. Withholding artificial life-support may be the best solution. We have probably all heard of cases where life-support was not used or else removed and the patient continued to live, or in some cases, to improve. If God so wills, no amount of medical technology will keep someone alive and no lack thereof will seal their death. God has recorded every day appointed to us before the first one began (Psalm 139:16).

It is important to recognize the uniqueness of each individual case. What seems right in one situation may not be so in another. It helps to discuss the possibilities before the crises. We need to discern if the person is saved, if the situation is hopeless, and if the response is passive. Most of all, we need to trust God to guide us and to have His way in the life of our loved one.

AIDS—How Should I Respond?

Experts say that AIDS will be the largest, most widespread, and most deadly disease *ever* known on earth. Its death toll will far surpass previous plagues. Even the black plague will seem light by comparison. The day is not far off when this scourge will reach into the church and each of us will know friends or relatives who are infected. Perhaps one or more in our midst will test positive. What do we do then? This disease was once confined to drug addicts and homosexuals, but it is now being found in what is usually considered the "straight" community. In fact, in the Central African Republic where I served as a missionary, AIDS is *primarily* passed by heterosexual contact, homosexual activity being very rare.

This is a current and growing problem and one we need to face up to. The problem of AIDS will not just go away and it will not just bypass our camp. There are two basic questions we need to deal with: 1) How do I keep from getting AIDS? And 2) How do I respond to an AIDS victim?

We want to be protected from this plague as much as possible and we desire to insulate our loved ones from its death blow. Is this possible to accomplish, and if so, how?

No one can make assurances that we will not come into contact with AIDS but we *can* take some definite measures to reduce the risk. We need to keep in mind that AIDS is not passed from one person to another by mere casual contact. We do not need to be paranoid and we do not need to avoid being in the same room with an AIDS victim. AIDS carries with it not only a death penalty but also a stigma as long as the person lives, even though the victim may have come in contact with the disease through no fault of his own (for example, receiving contaminated blood). Our goal is not to avoid AIDS victims but to avoid becoming a victim of AIDS. There are several suggestions which, if followed, should greatly reduce our risk.

If you remain faithful to your spouse and your spouse remains faithful to you, there is a very small chance of contacting AIDS. In the USA, this disease is still primarily transmitted through homosexual or bisexual intercourse.

Suppose that the penalty for stealing was to have your hands cut off and that we lived in a society where more and more people were missing hands. Now some of them may be missing hands due to an industrial accident or car wreck, but the most common reason would be stealing. How could you avoid losing your hands? The most important step to take would be one of abstinence—keep from stealing.

Homosexual and bisexual activity carry with them a number of penalties. One of those built-in penalties is AIDS. I believe that this is part of what Paul meant when he wrote the following words to the Romans:

> For since the creation of the world His invisible attributes are clearly seen, being understood by the things that are made, even His eternal power and Godhead, so that they are without excuse, because, although they knew God, they did not glorify Him as God, nor were thankful, but became futile in their thoughts, and their foolish hearts were darkened. Professing to be wise, they became fools, and changed the glory of the incorruptible God into an image made like corruptible man—and birds and four-footed animals and creeping things. Therefore God also gave them up to uncleanness, in the lusts of their hearts, to dishonor their bodies among themselves, who exchanged the truth of God for the lie, and worshiped and served the creature rather than the Creator, who is blessed forever. Amen. For this reason

God gave them up to vile passions. For even their women exchanged the natural use for what is against nature. Likewise also the men, leaving the natural use of the woman, burned in their lust for one another, men with men committing what is shameful, and receiving in themselves the penalty of their error which was due.

(Romans 1:20–27)

If the penalty for stealing is losing your hands, then to retain your hands you must abstain from stealing. If the penalty for homosexual activity is AIDS, then to keep from getting AIDS you must abstain from such activity.

There are some questions which arise from connecting AIDS with Paul's statement in Romans 1:20–27. If, for instance, AIDS was what was "due" (v. 27) to homosexuals as a penalty for that debased behavior, then why are only *some* and why only *now* in history instead of all through the years? There are two answers. First of all, we must reckon with God's grace. Certainly they all deserve to have the penalty of God's wrath (just as all of *us* do), but God is gracious. Secondly, AIDS is just *part* of the penalty. There have always been other consequences in the areas of medical and emotional health as well as the destruction of family life. Perhaps the penalty is getting worse due to the increase of open and flagrant homosexual activity and our drawing near to the end of time (2 Tim. 3:1–4).

Another question is: Why should *this* sin be singled out for such a penalty? We all sin and we all deserve God's penalty. Our wonder should be redefined to cause us to ask instead: How could God be so merciful as to not destroy us all right now? The amazing thing is not that God inflicts a penalty, but rather that He withholds the penalty we deserve. As David wrote: "He has not dealt with us according to our sins, nor punished us according to our iniquities" (Psalm 103:10). As to *why* this sin may have been singled out, it is hard to say. Throughout history God has been very clear and definite in His dislike for and penalty of sexual sins. An example is found in 1 Corinthians 6:18: "Flee sexual immorality. Every sin that a man does is outside the body, but he who commits sexual immorality sins against his own body."

By keeping ourselves pure until marriage, and faithful in marriage, we can greatly reduce the possibility of ever contracting AIDS.

203

A second step we can take is also one of abstinence: avoid using drugs. We are not talking here about medication which has been prescribed by a physician and is necessary for the treatment of an illness. We have in mind those drugs which are used for a "recreational" purpose. All of these must, of course, be avoided by a believer. There is a particular risk involved for those who use needles to inject their drugs and by the sharing or multiple use of needles. By avoiding both the drugs and the needles, another major contributor of AIDS can be kept out of our lives.

Though the percentage is small, there is also a threat of being infected with AIDS by receiving donated blood. As the number of AIDS infected victims increases in our society the amount of contaminated blood available for donation to those in need will likewise increase. Since AIDS is passed by the blood, this could pose a real threat. It must be noted, however, that the cases of AIDS caused by infected donated blood are rare. We do not need to panic, but we should take some precautionary measures.

If you must receive donated blood, it would be wise to limit the circle of possible donors. Time may not allow for selectivity, but when it does, request the needed blood from friends you know well and from members of your church. This will greatly reduce the risk of receiving contaminated blood. Even then, it is always possible that one of your friends may be infected and not know it. Whose blood would you rather have, though, your friend's or that drawn from Mr. X?

Our churches need to be aware of the potential dangers and we should be ready and willing to respond when one of our members is in need of our assistance—even if that means some of our blood. Surely, we should be willing to donate some of ours for a brother or sister in the Lord.

A very prevalent concern is how to avoid contracting AIDS. Sexual purity and faithfulness to your spouse, avoidance of drugs and needles, and an attempt to personally select donors in the event you need blood combine to greatly reduce the risk. Although we may not contract AIDS, we will most likely come in contact with AIDS victims. How should we respond?

Our response will probably be somewhat contingent on *how* the individual contracted AIDS. If they were infected through a secondary source (transfusion, etc.), then our reaction would probably tend to be different from what we would have in the case of someone who was infected due to primary involvement (i.e., homosexual activity). Much of our response, however, should be very much the same.

In the case where an individual is infected with AIDS due to no fault of his own, such as in the case of a transfusion, we should respond to them as we would to anyone who had a terminal illness. If they are not saved, what they need most of all is a right relationship with the Lord. Whether they are saved or not, they need our compassion. In addition, they may need our help in physical needs, emotional needs, monetary needs, and spiritual needs.

The day may be upon us when such people are in our congregations and perhaps even in our own families. We do not have the option of not loving them. We will need to reach out to them. We will need to show them that Jesus cares and so do we. We may have to overcome prejudice and paranoia among our own friends, but we cannot allow obstacles to hinder us from ministry.

Let's now consider a case in which the individual became infected due to homosexual activity or through the sharing of a needle in partaking of drugs. Our initial reaction might well be that they have received what they deserved, which is certainly correct. However, taking the beam out of our own eye first may cause us to see more clearly and to realize that we are equally deserving. Our hands are not clean.

I would suggest that our response to such people should be very much as we might respond to an individual suffering from a terminal liver disease due to drinking. There are some parallels since both cases involve diseases which are terminal and which were caused by sinful activity. What kind of response, then, would that involve?

The primary need they have is for salvation. Sure, their sin is great—but it is not more than the price paid to cover it! As Paul reminds us: ". . . where sin abounded, grace abounded much more" (Romans 5:20). Also, as in the first case, they will need compassion and they will need to be ministered to.

As mentioned earlier, there are some differences in how we will respond depending on how the individual contracted AIDS. In the present situation, where the infection is due to sinful activity, there must be repentance (this is obviously not the case with one who was infected due to no fault of their own). Where there is no repentance, neither will there be salvation. Also, it will be difficult for us to really minister to such an individual.

We cannot allow the pendulum to swing the other way to the point that we accept not only the individual but also his activity. We must not condone the sin or give the impression that we lightly esteem it. Loving an alcoholic does not mean that we love alcohol or promote its usage. Witnessing to an AIDS victim and demonstrating compassion are worthy goals. Condoning their sin or lifestyle would only make matters worse for them and would hurt our testimony

We would rather not have to face the issue of AIDS, but in this day that is not a realistic option. We need to both face it and respond in a godly way. In many cases God may be allowing us the privilege of ministering in His name, demonstrating His compassion, and above all, sharing the great news of Christ. May our Lord grant us much wisdom and discernment in the coming days!

PERSECUTION—HOW SHOULD I RESPOND?

There are laws in the United States and other Western nations which help to protect us from open and flagrant forms of persecution. Laws, however, do not stop the forces of evil. Satan and his band have simply been forced to adopt more subtle means. Christians are not thrown out of schools; they are often ridiculed for their beliefs instead. Believers are not fired for their religious convictions (at least not officially) but they may be overlooked for a promotion. In many cases a Christian is not permitted to talk about God while a pagan is freely allowed to blaspheme and to curse using God's name in vain. The A.C.L.U. has no lawsuits against Halloween decorations, yet they fight against Christian Christmas decorations.

We would like to ask the same questions as Senator Jeremiah Denton produced on the floor of the U.S. Senate when the subject was discussed; How is it that high school students can address God profanely in the hallway, but not reverently in the classroom? Why must they pledge allegiance to a nation under God, yet be denied permission to discuss the nature of that God? By what logic can students meet after school to hear the philosophies of Plato, Marx, and Hitler, but not Moses, Paul, or Jesus?

Persecution is not something that might happen, but something that does happen. I would like to suggest three responses to persecution: 1) determine the cause, 2) determine the source, and 3) determine to follow Christ's example.

The first step we need to take is to determine the cause. The cause is not always readily apparent. I have had people complain to me about being persecuted who were convinced that it was brought on because of their Christian stand. Unfortunately, in many cases the employer, co-workers, fellow students, etc., did not even realize the person in question was a born-again believer! The "persecution" may be across the board, i.e., *everyone* is being mistreated. Another possibility is that the cause is more directly related to the poor performance, behavior, or personality of the one who feels persecuted. In other words, the persecuted one may be "asking for it" in the world's view. Peter, who had very much to say about persecution, gave us these words:

> For this is commendable, if because of conscience toward God one endures grief, suffering wrongfully. For what credit is it if, when you are beaten for your faults, you take it patiently? But when you do good and suffer for it, if you take it patiently, this is commendable before God.
>
> (1 Peter 2:19–20)

If you are "beaten for your faults" you cannot rightly call that persecution. Sad to say, I have known some pretty obnoxious Christians and others who were lazy or incompetent. These people sometimes faced difficulties in the job place, not because they were Christians, but because they brought it on themselves. Therefore, when you sense that you are being persecuted, it would be wise to examine your life and lifestyle to see if *you* are the cause.

Genuine persecution is, of course, suffering at the hands of others even though you do not deserve such ill treatment. Perhaps you are indeed suffering "for righteousness' sake." Peter also tells us how to respond in such a case:

> But even if you should suffer for righteousness' sake, you are blessed. "And do not be afraid of their threats, nor be troubled." But sanctify

the Lord God in your hearts, and always be ready to give a defense to everyone who asks you a reason for the hope that is in you, with meekness and fear; having a good conscience, that when they defame you as evildoers, those who revile your good conduct in Christ may be ashamed. For it is better, if it is the will of God, to suffer for doing good than for doing evil.

(1 Peter 3:14–17)

The words "even if" in verse 14 comprise what is termed a "fourth class condition" in Greek, which indicates that this is an unlikely situation. It is possible, but not likely, that someone would suffer *because* he is leading a righteous life (see also Romans 13:1–7). It is more likely that someone would suffer because of his relationship to Christ. Satan is not as disturbed by our good deeds (in fact, he would like for men to depend on them for salvation) as he is by our relation to Christ. He is anti-good but he is primarily anti-Christ. But in this passage, Peter concedes the point: even if you *do* suffer for righteousness' sake, here is how to respond . . . (vv 15–16).

Our responsibility is first of all to sanctify (make holy or set apart as special) the Lord God in our hearts. Secondly, we are to witness. We are to "give a defense" as to our righteousness, which is, of course, based completely on our relationship with Jesus and His grace in our lives (Phil. 3:9). That witness is further defined as being selective: "to everyone who asks you a reason for the hope that is in you." It is not that we are only to witness to those who ask us to do so (a rare case indeed!). The point is that, in a case of persecution, those who are anti-Christ will not receive your testimony anyway; they may persecute you all the more and it would also constitute a casting of your pearls before swine (Matt. 7:6). But for those who inquire about your hope, explain to them about "Christ in you, the hope of glory" (Col. 1:27).

We are further instructed on *how* to give this witness: "with meekness and fear." In addition, our life must match our witness; we must live what we believe (v. 16).

Having determined the cause, we next need to determine the source. Our reaction to the persecution will be somewhat colored by this bit of information. We will consider three possible sources: unbelievers, spouse, and believers.

A natural source of persecution in any realm is from those who believe otherwise. We see it in small measure, for instance, when one political candidate blasts his opponent or when a feminist attacks a chauvinist (or vice versa). We can expect the same to be true in the case of belief in God. Those who do not believe are divided from those who do believe. Not only is their belief system different, but their values, priorities, perspectives, and lifestyles are radically opposed to committed Christians. It may be, therefore, that one would be persecuted because the source of that persecution is an unbeliever. Peter wrote:

> If you are reproached for the name of Christ, blessed are you, for the Spirit of glory and of God rests upon you. On their part He is blasphemed, but on your part He is glorified. But let none of you suffer as a murderer, a thief, an evildoer, or as a busybody in other people's matters. Yet if anyone suffers as a Christian, let him not be ashamed, but let him glorify God in this matter.
>
> (1 Peter 4:14–16)

To be persecuted for the name of Christ is a blessing (v. 14)! The persecution itself is not a blessing, but rather such a close identification with Christ is something we all should desire to have. An added bonus is that this gives opportunity to glorify God (14b, 16b). Jesus explained that those who are persecuted because of Him are in good company.

> Blessed are you when they revile and persecute you, and say all kinds of evil against you falsely for My sake. Rejoice and be exceedingly glad, for great is your reward in heaven, for so they persecuted the prophets who were before you.
>
> (Matthew 5:11–12)

If we are closely aligned with Christ, we can expect persecution because of that relationship. Although the physical body of Christ is no longer on this planet to serve as a target to His enemies, the Body of Christ, meaning His Church, makes a large and inviting target. Since they hate Him, they will hate you. Your identification with Him makes you fair game for them. The same source (unbelievers) that would attack the Shepherd will not flinch from attacking the sheep. As Jesus said:

If the world hates you, you know that it hated Me before it hated you. If you were of the world, the world would love its own. Yet because you are not of the world, but I chose you out of the world, therefore the world hates you. Remember the word that I said to you, "A servant is not greater than his master." If they persecuted Me, they will also persecute you. If they kept My word, they will keep yours also.

(John 15:18–20)

How should we respond to those who persecute us? Jesus lists in a very clear and simple fashion how He wants us to respond. He tells us to love them, bless them, do good to them, and pray for them (Matt. 5:44). He did not say it would be easy. In fact, I have found it to be utterly impossible to accomplish without His strength and enablement. He also did not say that there was an option. There is no plan B in case we do not want plan A. Because it is difficult does not reduce our responsibility; rather it increases our dependence.

God can do amazing things in the life of an unbeliever who persecutes His people. Of Paul it was said: "He who formerly persecuted us now preaches the faith which he once tried to destroy" (Gal. 1:23). Wouldn't it be great if the one who is persecuting you became your brother or sister in Christ? God can do it.

Another source of persecution is the family. Perhaps the most prevalent and heart-rending situation involves the persecution which comes from a spouse. Marriage is a divine institution and is the first and foundational unit ordained by God (Gen. 2:24). Satan knows this and delights to be in the home-wrecking business.

A believer should not marry an unbeliever (2 Cor. 6:14–17). Numerous heart-breaking stories result from not heeding this instruction. The same kind of situation may develop when two unbelievers are married and only one of them becomes a believer. The result is the same—lack of spiritual harmony. This circumstance can result in the persecution of the believer.

Peter addresses the issue from the vantage point of a believing wife married to an unbelieving husband. He gives the following instruction:

Wives, likewise, be submissive to your own husbands, that even if some do not obey the word, they, without a word, may be won by the conduct of their wives, when they observe your chaste conduct accompanied by fear. Do not let your adornment be merely outward; arranging the hair, wearing gold, or putting on fine apparel; rather let it be the hidden person of the heart, with the incorruptible beauty of a gentle and quiet spirit, which is very precious in the sight of God. For in this manner, in former times, the holy women who trusted in God also adorned themselves, being submissive to their own husbands, as Sarah obeyed Abraham, calling him lord, whose daughters you are if you do good and are not afraid with any terror.

(1 Peter 3:1–6)

Although the passage is directed to women, men can also profit from its teaching. Men will not follow the same pattern but they can employ the same principle. God expects us to respond with the right trust, the right kind of spirit, and the right order in the home.

A third source of persecution is from other believers. Satan will pit us one against the other in order to split our unity, tear down the house from the inside, and destroy our testimony and usefulness. It is amazing to me what petty things we as Christians will argue over while we let the weightier issues go.

How is it that we could be so led astray? James asks: "Where do wars and fights come from among you?" and then answers his own question with "Do they not come from your desires for pleasures that war in your members?" (James 4:1). This seeking after worldly pleasures (James 4:2–4), judging our brothers (James 4:11–12), and seeking our own will instead of God's will (James 4:13–16) results in divisions, lack of love and ministry toward one another, and even persecutions of one another. As James said, "My brethren, these things ought not to be so" (James 3:10).

Our response depends on whether we are the offending party or the offended party. If we realize we have been offending a brother, it is our obligation to go to him and make it right with him. We are to seek reconciliation (Matt. 5:23–24). If we have been offended by another believer, then we are to follow the procedure outlined for us by the Lord in Matthew 18. That procedure reads:

Moreover if your brother sins against you, go and tell him his fault between you and him alone. If he hears you, you have gained your brother. But if he will not hear, take with you one or two more, that 'by the mouth of two or three witnesses every word may be established.' And if he refuses to hear them, tell it to the church. But if he refuses even to hear the church, let him be to you like a heathen and a tax collector. Assuredly, I say to you, whatever you bind on earth will be bound in heaven, and whatever you loose on earth will be loosed in heaven. Again I say to you that if two of you agree on earth concerning anything that they ask, it will be done for them by My Father in heaven. For where two or three are gathered together in My name, I am there in the midst of them.

(Matthew 18:15–20)

There is no excuse for bitterness and strife. We are to love one another just like Jesus loves us (John 15:12). We are to forgive one another, and to this degree: ". . . just as God in Christ also forgave you" (Eph. 4:32). We are to have unity (Phil. 2:2), we are to have humility (Phil. 2:3), we are to look out for the needs of others (Phil. 2:4), and we are to be like Christ (Phil 2:5–8). Persecution of one believer by another is sin. "Therefore let us pursue the things which make for peace and the things by which one may edify another" (Rom. 14:19).

The first step is to determine the cause of the persecution. The second step is to determine the source of the persecution. While both of the steps are important, it is the third step which is essential, and that is: determine to follow Christ's example.

The clearest declaration of our Lord's will and example for us in this regard is found in 1 Peter:

For to this you were called, because Christ also suffered for us, leaving us an example, that you should follow His steps: who committed no sin, nor was deceit found in His mouth; who, when He was reviled, did not revile in return; when He suffered, He did not threaten, but committed Himself to Him who judges righteously; who Himself bore our sins in His own body on the tree, that we, having died to sins, might live for righteousness—by whose stripes you were healed.

(1 Peter 2:21–24)

No matter what others do, we are held accountable for our own actions (Romans 14:10–12). Christ's reaction to persecution may be summed up in these words: "Who committed no sin." That is our example, not how someone got even or settled a score. Christ did not commit a sin but instead "committed Himself to Him who judges righteously." God will even the score and, more importantly, He will take care of us. He will let nothing happen to us beyond His will. "Therefore, let those who suffer according to the will of God commit their souls to Him in doing good, as to a faithful Creator" (1 Peter 4:19).

SHOULD I TAKE ANOTHER BELIEVER TO COURT?

George was retired from farming and still had some equipment lying around which had been unused for several years. Tom received permission to use some of the equipment which subsequently broke in usage. Tom offered to pay $1,000 for the damage. George insisted on $2,000. Neither would budge. It came to trial. Both men were Christian leaders in their church and community. Another believer came to me with a dilemma—he was asked to testify at the trial. What should be done?

Ralph and Martha had a medium-sized family business. Another family in their church was looking for an investment opportunity. Proposals were discussed and plans were made. Finally, an investment agreement was reached. Based upon that agreement, Ralph and Martha expanded their operation and committed themselves financially. The other couple suddenly backed out and moved to another state. Ralph and Martha stood to lose much, perhaps even their business. Should they sue?

These are true situations which are, unfortunately, not uncommon in the Church. They raise a current and crucial question, should one believer take another believer to court? Our first response, on a human level, might well depend on whether we are the ones suffering loss or not. It's kind of like asking a happily married couple if they think divorce is okay. They would probably respond negatively. The same couple, given different circumstances (like an affair), might change their view. But whether divorce is legitimate or not should not be based on how we feel at the moment, or how circumstances are affecting us. We need the solid foundation of the Word, which is unaffected by time or society or circumstances or feelings, to be our guide. The question, therefore, must be answered by what God says and not by how we feel at the moment.

The Lord has given us some clear instruction on the matter. In Paul's first letter to the Corinthians, he addressed the issue by giving four reasons why one believer cannot take another believer to court. Because this passage is so crucial, we need to look at it in its entirety and then examine the four reasons Paul brings out.

The passage reads as follows:

> Dare any of you, having a matter against another, go to law before the unrighteous, and not before the saints? Do you not know that the saints will judge the world? And if the world will be judged by you, are you unworthy to judge the smallest matters? Do you not know that we shall judge angels? How much more, things that pertain to this life? If then you have judgments concerning things pertaining to this life, do you appoint those who are least esteemed by the church to judge? I say this to your shame. Is it so, that there is not a wise man among you, not even one, who will be able to judge between his brethren? But brother goes to law against brother, and that before unbelievers! Now therefore, it is already an utter failure for you that you go to law against one another. Why do you not rather accept wrong? Why do you not rather let yourselves be cheated? No, you yourselves do wrong and cheat, and you do these things to your brethren! Do you not know that the unrighteous will not inherit the kingdom of God? Do not be deceived. Neither fornicators, nor idolaters, nor adulterers, nor homosexuals, nor sodomites, nor thieves, nor covetous, nor drunkards, nor revilers, nor extortioners will inherit the kingdom of God. And such were some of you. But you were washed, but you were sanctified, but you were justified in the name of the Lord Jesus and by the Spirit of our God.
>
> (1 Corinthians 6:1–11)

There is nothing more disturbing than seeing two believers fight. It dishonors God; it destroys the lives and testimonies of those involved and it very often disrupts the church. The only one who gains from it is Satan. It is good to stop and examine whose side we are on and to consider seriously why we cannot take another believer to court.

As we look at Paul's instructions, we find that we cannot take another believer to court because of who we are. In the first two verses, we discover that we are saints and we are judges.

We are saints. That does not mean that our actions are perfect but rather that we have been declared righteous or perfect (Heb. 10:14) since our sins are covered by the blood of the Lamb.

Since a holy God accepts and forgives you, surely you can (and must) accept and forgive one another (Eph. 4:32). Christ died for that person you are thinking of taking to court. That believer belongs to the King and so do you. Both of you are declared to be "saints" (1 Cor. 1:2) by God's grace. Neither of you deserves it. Since you belong to the King, you must live by His rules and His standards, which are much higher than the world's standards. One saint has no business taking another saint to a worldly court.

We are also judges. We shall preside (the word also means to reign or rule) over the world as judges (see also Rev. 20:4; Dan. 7:21–27; 2 Tim. 2:12; Rev. 2:26–27; 3:21). If God is going to entrust us with such a responsibility, Paul argues, surely we ought to be able to judge among ourselves now. It is a disgrace to submit another believer to the judgment of the world which shall be judged by him. Besides, who has the better understanding and wisdom, a believer or an unbeliever?

We shall also judge angels (v. 3; 2 Pet. 2:4; Jude 6; Heb. 2:5–9). That will be an awesome responsibility. Since this is true, as Paul asks, ". . . how much more, things that pertain to this life?" Surely we as believers should be able to judge among ourselves and to discern rightly the issues of this present life. It is a shame to stoop to the world's level.

Secondly, we cannot take another believer to court because the court is of another kingdom. Read again verses 4–6. A major problem with submitting another believer to the world's court system is that it is "before unbelievers" (v. 6). According to Colossians 1:12–13 and 1 Peter 2:9–10, believers, by virtue of their new position in Christ, are no longer members of the Kingdom of Darkness (to which every unbeliever belongs) but have been made members of the Kingdom of Light. It is a gross error for two members of the Kingdom of Light to bring their case to the Kingdom of Darkness for judgment (2 Cor. 6:14–16). How can one who belongs to Christ ask one who belongs to Satan to judge a matter for him against his Christian brother? Even if the judge or arbitrator is a believer, the civic code to which he is bound is of the world.

This does not mean that courts are bad or evil, nor that lawyers are necessarily corrupt, nor that we should shun or ignore the legal system. We are grateful for the laws of our land and for their enforcement. We must remember, though, that the purpose of law is to insure peace and safety to all, and only those who break the law need fear being brought to judgment (Romans 13:1–7). The purpose of the legal system is not to enable you to sue your spiritual brother or sister. There are times when issues must be settled between believers. If the two parties in question cannot settle the dispute between themselves, they should ask for other believers to arbitrate (Matt. 18:15–20). Differences between believers should be resolved by believers. As John MacArthur put it so well:

> If two Christian parties cannot agree between themselves, they should ask fellow Christians to settle the matter for them, and be willing to abide by that decision. The poorest equipped believer, who seeks the counsel of God's Word and Spirit, is much more competent to settle disagreements between fellow believers than is the most highly trained and experienced unbelieving judge who is devoid of divine truth. Because we are in Christ, Christians rank above the world and even above angels. And by settling our own disputes, we give a testimony of our resources and of our unity, harmony, and humility before the world. When we go to public court, our testimony is the opposite.[10]

Another reason we cannot take another believer to court is because of our calling. We are called to do good, not evil; to bless, not curse, and to pursue after peace (1 Peter 3:9–11). We are told to ". . . be of one mind, having compassion for one another; love as brothers, be tenderhearted, be courteous . . ." (1 Peter 3:8). That kind of calling should lead us to suffer wrong rather than to insist on our "rights" at the expense of our brother and our testimony. That is why Paul writes:

Now therefore, it is already an utter failure for you that you go to law against one another. Why do you not rather accept wrong? Why do you not rather let yourselves be defrauded? No, you yourselves do wrong and defraud, and you do these things to your brethren!

(1 Corinthians 6:7–8)

If we seek those things which are above and if we set our minds and our affections on heavenly things rather than earthly things (Col. 3:1–2), then we would realize that it is better to lose physically or monetarily, if the will of God be so, than to lose spiritually. It is better to lose a case than to lose a brother.

By taking our case to other believers or to the church does not necessarily mean that we will lose our property or rights. Taking our case to the world's court, however, means instant and utter failure (1 Cor. 6:7), regardless of the legal outcome.

Finally, we cannot take another believer to court because we belong to God (1 Cor. 6:9–11, 19–20). Paul begins this section with a description of the world (vv. 9–10). They have no part in God's kingdom. Do we really want *them* to judge us? Next, Paul reminds us that "such were some of you," lest we be too high-minded. He marks the notable difference, however, by adding: "But you were washed . . . ." Since we belong to God, we are forgiven and we are not to be like the world. This is not only a description of us, but of every believer. Paul's closing comments in this chapter (vv. 19–20) also hit home; our body is the temple of the Holy Spirit. If that is true of us, it is also true of our brethren. Do you really want to drag a temple of the Holy Spirit before an ungodly world system? That is not how you can "glorify God in your body and in your spirit, which are God's" (1 Cor. 6:20).

The bottom line comes down to our priorities and our trust. We need to trust in God and not in money. God will honor those who trust Him. Our priorities do not have to say that our money, our jobs, our business, etc., are unimportant; but they do say that our Lord, our testimonies, and our brothers are more important.

DEATH—THE FINAL QUESTION, THE LAST ENEMY

"Death is swallowed up in victory"

1 Cor. 15:54

The topic of death is an uncomfortable one, especially for unbelievers. Death carries with it a certain dark mystery, a degree of uncertainty, and a measure of apprehensiveness. Even for those who are sure about where they are going, there may be some dread about the trip. Most of us have a desire to escape pain. Death is not to be thought of as a pleasant experience.

When we do face up to the reality of death, a number of questions come to mind, some of which are: What is death? Is death our enemy? Is death inevitable? What should be the believer's view of death?

What is death? To answer that question from a medical or scientific perspective is beyond the scope of this book and the expertise of the author. We will, however, try to answer the question from a biblical perspective.

One writer, in attempting to define death from the viewpoint of a believer, wrote the following poem:

What is Death?
What is death? Oh, what is death?

221

'Tis the snapping of the chain—
'Tis the breaking of the bowl—
'Tis relief from every pain—
'Tis freedom to the soul—
'Tis the setting of the sun
To rise again tomorrow,
A brighter course to run
Nor sink again to sorrow.
Such is death! Yes, such is death!

What is death? Oh! What is death?
'Tis slumber to the weary—
'Tis rest to the forlorn—
'Tis shelter to the dreary—
'Tis peace amid the storm—
'Tis the entrance to our home—
'Tis the passage to that God
Who bids His children come,
When their weary course is trod.
Such is death! Yes, such is death.

Unknown

Often when we ask the question, "what is death?" we really mean to ask, "*when* is death?" A person is alive one second and dead the next—what changed? What constitutes death? The Bible gives us a very simple answer from the pen of Paul. To summarize what he wrote to the Corinthians, death occurs when the spirit leaves the body. In context we read:

For we know that if our earthly house, this tent, is destroyed, we have a building from God, a house not made with hands, eternal in the heavens. For in this we groan, earnestly desiring to be clothed with our habitation which is from heaven, if indeed, having been clothed, we shall not be found naked. For we who are in this tent groan, being burdened, not because we want to be unclothed, but further clothed, that mortality may be swallowed up by life. Now He who has prepared us for this very thing is God, who also has given us the Spirit as a guarantee. Therefore we are always confident, knowing that while we are at home in the body we are absent from the Lord. For we walk by faith, not by sight. We are confident, yes, well pleased rather to be absent from the body and to be present with the Lord.

(2 Corinthians 5:1–8)

There is no limbo. If our spirit is inside our earthly tent (our body), then we are alive. The moment our spirit ceases to reside within us, we are "present with the Lord." Death, then, is the absence of the spirit from the body. The moment of death occurs when the spirit exits the body. This is furthermore a process which will occur only once for each individual (Heb. 9:27), thus refuting the idea of reincarnation.

Whereas physical death is the separation of the spirit from the body, spiritual death is the separation of the spirit from God (Romans 6:23). That is why anyone who is outside of Christ will not see the kingdom of God (John 3:1–7).

For the believer, however, death is but the releasing of the spirit to the presence of the Lord. This thought is expressed on a grave in ancient Greece in this way:

Zosime, a slave in body alone,
Has now found freedom.

On a tombstone of a certain Solomon Peas, who was buried in London, one can read:

Beneath these clouds and beneath these trees,
Lies the body of Solomon Peas;
This is not Peas; it is only his pod;
Peas has shelled out and gone home to God!

Is death our enemy? Since death results in our presence with our Lord, should we view death as a friend instead of an enemy?

Death *is* our enemy. The Bible says that "the last enemy that will be destroyed is death" (1 Cor. 15:26). That time is still future. Death will be cast into the lake of fire after the thousand year reign of Christ on earth (Rev. 20:14). Until then, it will take its toll.

The reason death is still our enemy is that the curse upon Adam (Gen. 3:19) is still in operation. None of us is without sin, and the curse

223

is upon us as well (Rom. 5;12). Also, it is the result of death, not the process of death, which brings us into God's presence. That we die is still a curse and still an enemy. What happens at the moment of death is another matter. For each believer, victory lies not in death, but beyond death, and we may say with Paul: "Thanks be to God, who gives us the victory through our Lord Jesus Christ" (1 Cor. 15:57).

Is death inevitable? As far as I know, the mortality rate among human beings of all sorts has been determined to be 100%! There is a saying that "nothing is sure but death and taxes." I have known of people who have evaded taxes, but nobody can evade death. We each have an appointment with death. As Hebrews 9:27–28a tells us: "And it is appointed for men to die once, but after this the judgment, so Christ was offered once to bear the sins of may," so will each man die physically once and only once. Also, just as Christ surely died, so each of us can surely expect to die.

There appears to be a loophole in this scheme. Will not those who are raptured escape death? We read of Enoch that he "walked with God; and he was not, for God took him" (Gen. 5:24). Elijah was suddenly taken up to heaven in a chariot of fire (2 Kgs. 2:11). A similar picture seems to be painted by Paul when he writes: "Then we who are alive and remain shall be caught up together with them in the clouds to meet the Lord in the air. And thus we shall always be with the Lord" (1 Thess. 4:17).

A key to understanding this is to recall our definition of death, i.e., when the spirit is separated from the body. I believe that this is still technically the case even in the event of rapture. What is different about the rapture is that the *process* of death is circumvented. The *fact* of death remains the same. These earthly bodies will never make it to heaven. This can be clearly seen from the following passage:

> Now this I say, brethren, that flesh and blood cannot inherit the kingdom of God; nor does corruption inherit incorruption. Behold, I tell you a mystery: We shall not all sleep, but we shall all be changed—in a moment, in the twinkling of an eye, at the last trumpet.
>
> For the trumpet will sound, and the dead will be raised incorruptible, and we shall be changed. For this corruptible must put on incorrup-

tion, and this mortal must put on immortality. So when this corruptible has put on incorruption, and this mortal has put on immortality, then shall be brought to pass the saying that is written: "Death is swallowed up in victory."

(1 Corinthians 15:50–54)

Notice especially that "flesh and blood cannot inherit the kingdom of God" (v. 50) and "we shall all be changed" (vv. 51–52). When this happens, *then* victory will be won over death (v. 54). The point is, this physical body will not live on for eternity in its present form. Had it not been for the curse, that would have been possible. But now the spirit must inhabit another body, one that has been made incorruptible and immortal. We must have a spiritual body for our spiritual destination (1 Cor. 15:42–44). We could say that this is merely a changing of our physical body into a spiritual body. This is true, but the very fact that this change must be made indicates that this physical body in its present form must be altered for its eternal destination.

In the long run there is very little difference. We may even say, practically speaking, that those who are raptured will not "experience" death as far as the process of death is concerned.

Death is inevitable. Our goal is not to evade death but to know where we will be on the other side. Those who know the Savior can safely say "we shall always be with the Lord" (1 Thess. 4:17).

What should be the believer's view of death? I have been surprised to find such a wide variety of views and feelings about death among believers. Many factors combine to give such divergent views: different levels of spiritual maturity, different degrees of proximity to death, how family and friends have reacted to death, and the amount of biblical knowledge one possesses on the subject, just to name a few. How we see death should be colored by our relationship with Christ and what death means to us in light of that relationship. The Apostle Paul put it simply: "For to me, to live is Christ, and to die is gain" (Phil. 1:21). The believer should see death as gain. We do not wish to be separated from our loved ones, but we long even more to be with our Lord. We do not desire to remain in this earthly shell, but rather long for that resurrected body. We do not want to continue to sin, but instead long for the day when sinning shall be no more. We look forward to the time of rest, absence

225

of sorrow, reuniting with loved ones, etc. To die is gain. But notice that Paul precedes that statement with another one just as important: "to live is Christ." It is the one who can say "to live is Christ" who can also say "to die is gain." Such a person could say:

Afterwards

Light after darkness, gain after loss
Strength after weakness, crown after cross,
Sweet after bitter, hope after fears
Home after wandering, praise after tears
Sheaves after sowing, sun after rain,
Sight after mystery, peace after pain
Joy after sorrow, calm after blast,
Rest after weariness, sweet rest at last
Near after distant, gleam after gloom,
Love after loneliness, life after tomb
After long agony, rapture of bliss—
Right was the pathway leading to this

Frances R. Havergal

The believer may face the enemy, death, with the confidence that Jesus has already secured the victory. We have life eternal and physical death cannot change that spiritual reality. Since this is true, Jesus was able to make the tremendous statement: "I am the resurrection and the life. He who believes in Me, though he may die, he shall live" (John 11:25).

I remember being called to the bedside of John Singley. John was on the verge of death. He could not speak but he could communicate by writing on my palm with his finger. John had recently accepted the gift of salvation through Jesus Christ. As I approached him, he took my hand and, smiling the most peaceful smile you can image, wrote H-E-A-V-E-N. Within moments he was there. John knew where he was going and he boarded that train for glory confident that his ticket had been paid in full.

Death should be viewed not as a state but as a doorway; not as a condition but as a channel. As David wrote: "Yea, though I walk through the valley of the shadow of death, I will fear no evil" (Ps. 23:4). We do not remain in the valley, we just walk through. Our eternal destiny as believers is not death but life.

It is said that when John Owen, the great Puritan pastor, lay on his deathbed, his secretary wrote (in his name) to a friend, "I am still in the land of the living." "Stop," said Owen. "Change that to say: I am yet in the land of the dying, but I hope soon to be in the land of the living."

God has determined exactly when each one's death will take place (Ps. 139:16). We should view death, then, as the final accomplishment of God's will for us. God counts that moment of death as very special; in fact He says: "Precious in the sight of the Lord is the death of His saints" (Ps. 116:15).

God has special and glorious things in store for His children when they arrive home. We read: "Eye has not seen, nor ear heard, nor have entered into the heart of man the things which God has prepared for those who love Him" (1 Cor. 2:9). Such a view leads us to say with C. C. White:

"I Cannot Think of Thee With Tears"

Beloved! I cannot wear for thee
The sigh of mourning as my dress,
For thou art keeping company
With unimagined happiness;

The light of dayspring in thine eyes,
Immortal health in every breath,
The splendor of thy summer skies—
All tell me Christ hath banished death.

The coronation of thy King
Awaits completion of the throng,
And all the choirs celestial bring
Their tributes for the triumph song.

I have an invitation too,
Which lights with hope our parted years,
And when I read its message through
I cannot think of thee with tears.

C. C. White

We have faced and will yet likely encounter many difficulties, adversities, trials, and struggles. The final enemy we will face is death. In death just as in life our victory is based not upon our own ability, but upon the power of God, and our hope does not rest in ourselves, but in the finished work of Christ. Between now and glory, no matter what our adversity, the heart of faith can say with Paul: "For I consider that the sufferings of this present time are not worthy to be compared with the glory which shall be revealed in us" (Romans 8:18).

Notes

[1] Roy R. Roberts, *Life in the Pressure Cooker: Studies in James* (Winona Lake, IN: BMH Books, 1977), p. 154.

[2] Richard Mayhue, "Are Anointing Services For Me?" in *Moody Monthly*, May 1989, p. 47.

[3] Nancy Gibbs, "Love and Let Die," in *Time*, Vol. 135, No. 12, March 19, 1990, p. 64.

[4] "Misericorde" in *Webster's II New Riverside University Dictionary* (Boston, MA: Houghton Mifflin, 1984).

[5] "Love and Let Die," p. 68

[6] Lewis B. Smedes, "A Bifocal Perspective," in *Christianity Today*, January 1985, p. 25.

[7] Dr. Thomas Elkins, "A Legacy of Life," in *Christianity Today*, January 1985, p. 23.

[8] "Love and Let Die," p. 70.

[9] "A Legacy of Life," p. 19.

[10] John MacArthur, *1 Corinthians,* in the MacArthur New Testament Commentary (Winona Lake, IN: BMH Books, 1984), p. 139.

To order additional copies of

GOLD UNDER
FIRE

Have your credit card ready and call:

1-877-421-READ (7323)

or please visit our web site at
www.pleasantword.com

Also available at:
www.amazon.com
and
www.barnesandnoble.com

www.growingingrace.net

LaVergne, TN USA
27 April 2010
180754LV00005B/29/A